To: ████████

From: ~~Mom and Dad (wrong)~~
~~Grandma and Grandpa~~

Christmas: 1990

MW01033401

HERITAGE CHRISTIAN CHURCH
1640 South Coy Road
Oregon, Ohio 43616

DINO KARTSONAKIS

WITH CECIL MURPHEY

AN AUTOBIOGRAPHY

Beyond the Glitz and Glamour

Dino

THOMAS NELSON PUBLISHERS

Published in Nashville, Tennessee, by Thomas Nelson, Inc., and
distributed in Canada by Lawson Falle, Ltd., Cambridge, Ontario.

Unless otherwise noted, the Bible version used in this
publication is THE NEW KING JAMES VERSION OF THE BIBLE.
Copyright © 1979, 1980, 1982, Thomas Nelson, Inc., Publishers.
Scripture quotations marked TLB are from *The Living Bible*
(Wheaton, Illinois: Tyndale House Publishers, 1971) and are
used by permission.

Library of Congress Cataloging-in-Publication Data

Kartsonakis, Dino.
    Dino : an autobiography : beyond the glitz and glamour / Dino
Kartsonakis with Cecil Murphey.
        p.   cm.
    ISBN 0-8407-7158-4
    1. Kartsonakis, Dino.   2. Pianist—United States—Biography.
I. Murphey, Cecil.   II. Title.
ML417.K3A3   1990
786.2′092—dc20   90–33138
[B]   CIP
                                                         MN

Printed in the United States of America.
1 2 3 4 5 6 7 — 95 94 93 92 91 90

*And those who are wise—the people of God—shall
shine as brightly as the sun's brilliance, and
those who turn many to righteousness will
glitter like stars forever.*

—Daniel 12:3, TLB

Contents

Chapter 1

THE PROMISE

My grandmother stared first at me and then at Mom before she whispered in Greek, "Look at that."

Mom was already gaping in total surprise. At age three, I wasn't aware of anything unusual taking place; my attention was focused on our new piano.

Days earlier, a friend of the family had given us an old upright piano. Mom, who loved to sing and pick out simple melodies on the keyboard, accepted it graciously and enthusiastically.

When we came home after church the following Sunday, my sister went into another room and Mom and YaYa, which is Greek for "Grandmother," went into the kitchen. I walked over to the piano. Using the forefinger of my right hand, I picked out the melody of the hymn "At the Cross," which we had sung earlier in church, and played it through two or three times.

Mom had heard me playing the melody and tiptoed up behind me to listen. Grandma was beside her. The two women were amazed and, of course, delighted.

Years later, Mom said that God spoke to her at that moment and she heard these words in her heart, *This is a talent I have given your son. This is how I will use Dino. He will bring joy and happiness and the good news through the piano.*

For a few seconds Mom didn't say a word. She had committed me to God at birth, and, already, God had shown her my future ministry.

Mom was the oldest of six children, all very talented. As children, they had enjoyed music and Greek dancing. My mother sang with a high soprano voice, although she was not professionally trained. Most Greeks love music and Mom was one of the finest and most colorful dancers at Greek festivities.

Because of her own love of music, I know Mom was thrilled when she saw me first play the piano. But that Sunday afternoon, as I started picking out the tune and playing at it like it was a game, Mom wisely said, "That's nice, Dino. Maybe one day you'll learn to play well." And she calmly returned to the kitchen.

I'm grateful that in my presence she never made anything big out of my playing. Years later I learned that the day Mom calmly returned to the kitchen, tears of joy were rolling down her cheeks. I discovered that my musical talent was a matter of much prayer and delight for both her and Grandma. My piano playing was the second miracle of my life they witnessed together. My birth had been the first.

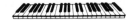

In the winter of 1941-1942, Helen (Eleni in Greek) Kartsonakis was on her way to Glad Tidings Tabernacle in

New York City. As she walked through driving sleet and rain with her four-year-old daughter, Helen's feet suddenly went out from under her, and she fell awkwardly to the pavement. Young Christina, whom the family called Chris, struggled to help her mother to her feet, and the two of them continued walking the remaining blocks to the Tabernacle.

Helen thought little of her fall, thankful she only had slight bruises. Although her body felt sore for several days and she was pregnant with her second child, Helen was a healthy woman. So she didn't think anymore about her accident. A few weeks later, on her way out of Glad Tidings, she stumbled again and fell down the steps.

From that time on, Helen began to have difficulties with her pregnancy. Her body constantly hurt and she complained, "I don't feel right." Helen finally went to Dr. Jeanopoulos, a Greek doctor who took care of most of the immigrants in the neighborhood. After the examination, he pronounced the ominous words, "There's no chance for the infant. This will be a stillbirth."

In tears, Helen left the doctor; she desperately wanted this child. All the way back to her apartment at Sixty-third and Amsterdam Avenue, she cried. She and her husband, John, had waited four years for a second child. "Oh, God," she pleaded between sobs, "please, please let this child live."

As soon as Helen walked into the house, she phoned her mother. Whenever the family faced upsets, sickness, or other problems, Christina Frudakis was the one they called. Her prayers seemed to bring results. Between tears and spasms of emotional pain, Helen poured out the terrible news.

"Eleni, you don't worry," Christina said. "I come now to see you."

"Thank you, Mama."

"Satan wants to take the life of this child from you, but God wants your baby to live. We'll pray and God will hear us because the devil isn't going to take this child!" Although Christina Frudakis was illiterate and still spoke only broken English, God communicated with her in visions and dreams and frequently gave her uncanny insight into spiritual problems.

Christina hurried to Eleni's house and went into the bedroom, where her daughter lay in bed, and began to pray into the night. Exhausted, she lay down next to her daughter to sleep. When she did, Christina had a vision of her daughter's living room. An evil presence crept inside the room and she could see that it wanted to hurt Helen. When she was later asked what the figure looked like, Christina said, "It was just a black figure of a man. But he was real, as real as if he had been sitting on the couch."

The black figure gripped Helen's waist, slowly tightening his grip, tormenting her mentally and causing her to feel excruciating pain.

"In the name of Jesus," Christina cried out as she watched this strange vision, "I rebuke Satan!" Again and again, Christina felt the chilling power of evil trying to destroy the unborn child.

"God, let this child live," she pleaded. "We dedicate this unborn infant to You. I promise that this child will serve You all the days of its life. I will do whatever I can to teach this little one to love You."

Christina rebuked Satan once more and abruptly the black figure let go of Helen, turned, and darted out of the apartment. This experience was so real to Christina that she later said she even heard his footsteps as he ran down the stairway. A calmness swept over Christina and she knew that God had heard her, that the baby would live, and that God would use this child's life in an extraordinary way.

In the morning, Christina asked Helen, "How are you feeling?"

Helen sighed, stretched, and then said, "You know, I do feel better. Better than I've felt in weeks."

"You will have a baby—a healthy one," Christina said. "God has shown me. He has also shown me that He has a special purpose for this child's life."

When Helen went back to Dr. Jeanopoulos for her next appointment, he exclaimed in utter amazement, "You're doing fine. The baby is alive and everything is normal."

A few weeks later on July 20, 1942, at St. Vincent's Hospital in Manhattan, Helen Kartsonakis gave birth to a healthy boy she named Constantino.

Later the family would simply call me Dino.

Chapter 2

THE
FIRST TOUCHES

Until I went into the army, my family lived in Manhattan at Sixty-third Street and Amsterdam Avenue, where Lincoln Center is located today. We lived on the third floor of a building with no elevator. My father owned the Lincoln Luncheonette on Sixty-sixth Street, and Mom worked there as a waitress. The small luncheonette didn't do a big business, but my father loved cooking. Dad probably gave away more food than he sold.

Although her personality differed from YaYa's, my mother had the same commitment to God and the same love of life my grandmother had. Like Grandma Frudakis, Mom had dark hair and dark eyes and was small and attractive. Mom always looked great because she had Grandma's flair for color and knew how to dress. From looking at Mom's clothes, people at Glad Tidings Tabernacle might have thought we were among the wealthiest of families, yet we didn't have a penny in the bank.

I never felt that Mom preached to me or forced me into the Christian faith. Her relationship with Jesus Christ was a vital part of her and it affected everything she said and did. She taught me about Jesus Christ from as far back as I can remember. So at age seven, I sincerely was able to say, "I believe in Jesus Christ." I can't recall a time when I *didn't* believe, only that at age seven I finally understood what Mom and YaYa had been teaching me.

When I was growing up, my dad didn't go to church and made no pretense about being a Christian. Not until he was older did he turn to Jesus Christ. However, he was one of the most principled men I've ever known. He had strong convictions about right and wrong, always wanted the best for Chris and me, and I knew he loved me.

Both my parents worked hard. Although they didn't make a lot of money, we lived as though we were the richest people in the world—not because we spent foolishly, but because of the spirit in our house. My parents never allowed Chris and me to feel we were poor. They, like YaYa, celebrated life and experienced pleasure in being alive, and they taught us to do the same. My parents and YaYa hoped and dreamed the best for us—they were people of vision. And as a result, I learned it was OK to have my own hopes and dreams.

One of my dreams was born during the years when I attended LaSalle Junior High School at Forty-seventh Street, right in the middle of the Broadway shows of Manhattan. I would often walk by the theaters during my lunch breaks. The whole scene fascinated me. I'd sneak into the theaters, some of which were being used for taping television programs. Once inside, I would watch a taping or sometimes see part of the rehearsal of a Broadway show. I'd sit, spellbound, and I'd find myself caught up in the action as if I were part of it.

"Hey, kid, out!"

Someone always figured out I didn't belong. As I heard the words, I'd move toward the door, walking as slowly as possible, trying to see as much as I could.

Everything I saw impressed me—the production, the technical aspects of filming—and I wished I could sit in there all day and not be thrown out.

One particular day as I left, I remember saying to myself, *Someday I'm going to be involved in television.* I didn't know how I'd be involved or what I'd do, but I knew I belonged before the cameras.

When I was a child, Mom didn't put me into the spotlight, but, after almost every church service, she did encourage me to keep picking out the melodies of new songs. As soon as we got home, I would head for the piano and pick out the music we had sung that morning. I was only four years old. I wasn't aware that I was talented or that God had given me a unique gift. I was just a little boy having fun, and my family encouraged me to play piano as I would any child's game.

Within a year, I learned to play just by watching the pianists at church. I was too short to reach the pedals, but within months, I could play with both hands. By then, I had picked up harmony and started adding chords.

Mom talked to Miss Florence Smith, the organist at Glad Tidings, about giving me lessons. An excellent music teacher, Miss Smith had studied under some of the most talented musicians of her day.

"He's too young for lessons," she said adamantly.

"But he is already playing. Really playing," Mom said. "With both hands."

"When he's older," Miss Smith replied. "I prefer to wait until they're eight. But if you still want him to have lessons when he's six, I'll talk to him. By then he'll be learning to read and write and will be easier to teach."

"But if you could see how quickly he has picked up chords . . ."

"Wait until he's older," she said firmly. "It'll be easier on me and on him."

When I was five years old, Miss Smith finally agreed to take me as a student. I now know she made a mistake. She should have taken me when I was three. By the time I was five, who needed Miss Smith? I had learned pretty well by observing the church pianists. And I had played in church a few times, though I wasn't particularly advanced. I think I knew just enough for people to say to Mom, "Isn't that cute?" But I had also locked myself into playing by ear and couldn't read a note. I didn't know notes existed—all I knew was what I heard. Even today it's easier for me to memorize by ear instead of reading the music. When I work on a selection for a recording with my producer and arranger, the music sticks indelibly in my mind—and unconscious thing that happens without any apparent effort.

Immediately, Miss Smith tried to teach me how to read the notes. "The notes, Dino." I can still hear her demanding voice. "Always read the notes. They were written like that for you to play just that way."

"Yes, Miss Smith," I answered. But I had already figured out how to get around her demand, which seemed silly and required a lot of work.

When she told me what she wanted me to learn for the next lesson, I would put on my best smile and ask, "Miss Smith, would you please play it for me? Just once, so I'll know what it sounds like."

"Of course," she always said. She then played my pieces and exercises one time. And once was all I needed.

"That was very nice," she would say the following week. "You must have practiced a long time on that."

I didn't actually lie, but for quite a while, I fooled her. However, Miss Smith finally discovered that God had given me a good ear for music memory. I don't recall how she caught on, but the day she did, Miss Smith blew up. "You are a hopeless case!" she said. "Just hopeless!"

Miss Smith phoned Mom and told her what I had been doing. She charged us two dollars a lesson—a lot for our family to pay in those days. "Save your two dollars for lessons and just let him play by ear," she said. "He refuses to learn how to read notes. He's hopeless. It'll be easier on you, and it won't be so frustrating for Dino and for me if he just stops taking lessons." Perhaps she was angry because it took her so long to figure out what I was doing—and that would reflect on her teaching. Or perhaps she simply didn't know what to do with my kind of talent.

"He'll learn to do it right," Mom protested and attempted to pacify her.

When I got home from my lesson, Mom said to me with real concern in her voice, "Dino, you've got to learn to read notes. Otherwise, Miss Smith is going to drop you as a student."

I relished the idea of being dropped because I didn't like practicing scales and repeating material I already knew well. But the situation wasn't that simple. Mom, Dad, and YaYa wanted me to learn to play properly. And as an obedient child in a Greek home, it didn't occur to me to disobey my parents.

"I'm sorry," I said. "I'll practice and I'll learn to read the notes. I promise."

Once I understood the intensity of my parents' desire for me to read music and to play the way Miss Smith taught me, I did what she told me. It wasn't easy for me to keep my promise. Sometimes I got bored and there were times when, like all children learning to play, I became frustrated. But every day after school I sat in front of that ancient upright piano and practiced.

Each Saturday morning, no matter what the weather, Mom, Chris, and I walked from our apartment at Sixty-third Street to 113th Street, where Miss Smith lived. Once inside Mom sat and crocheted while I played. That was her way of saying to me silently, "Dino, do it right."

That happened a long time ago, and I have not taken lessons in many years. Now I'm married and a parent myself. Yet once in a while, when I sit at my piano and practice for a concert, I close my eyes and see Mom sitting in Miss Smith's stuffed chair, her crocheting in her lap. The dark eyes stare at me and I hear her saying, "Dino, do it right."

Chapter 3

THE POWERFUL
YAYA

From before I was born until the day she died, YaYa lived alone in her small apartment on the fifth floor at Forty-third Street and Ninth Avenue. The building where she lived housed a fish market on the street floor and had no elevator. YaYa climbed those five flights of stairs every day. No matter how many times we tried to persuade her to move, she just smiled at us and said, "This is home." She never left her little apartment.

Christina Frudakis arrived in the United States from Greece as a young married woman. (Grandpa left her a few years later.)

One Sunday morning in 1937, when Christina was walking down Manhattan's Thirty-third Street, she saw a church building with a neon-lit cross high up on the building. Like most people she knew, Christina was Greek Orthodox. But for some reason she never explained, Christina walked inside Glad Tidings Tabernacle and sat down. Unable to read, she couldn't tell from the hymnals or bulletins what type of church she had entered (though she knew it was not

Greek Orthodox). Yet she immediately felt God's presence in that building as she had never felt it in any other church. *Ah, yes,* she said to herself, *God is in this place.* She was the first of the family members to discover Glad Tidings Tabernacle, which became both a pillar and a haven for our family. Glad Tidings Tabernacle had emerged as one of the most influential chuches in the Assemblies of God. With a membership exceeding twelve hundred, the congregation had a sense of mission to the whole world, coupled with the vision to reach the people in the neighborhood. Through the pastors, Robert and Marie Brown, Glad Tidings was touching the lives of those in the community.

Although she couldn't speak English, Christina sat attentively during the service, aware of the presence of God. The people were different from those she had seen in worship at the Greek Orthodox church she had gone to all her life. Everywhere she looked, she saw individuals filled with a joy she had never experienced or even known was possible.

Christina returned to Glad Tidings the following week. And every Sunday after that, she was there, enjoying the divine presence she felt and the joy she sensed that first time.

YaYa was a tower of strength to the entire family and her life bore powerful witness to God's love at work. One of her remarkable strengths was her consistency in influencing me, praying for me, and committing me to God. I grew up with the understanding that she only wanted me to honor God in whatever I chose to do.

A native of the Greek island Crete, YaYa resembled Golda Meir, with her black hair tied in a bun and her olive complexion. I particularly remember that YaYa's enthusiasm for life showed through her black sparkling eyes. And she had one of the most joyful laughs I've ever heard. A deeply spiritual woman, Grandma Frudakis still enjoyed life and didn't think Christians ought to live dull, boring lives.

YaYa had a flair for color, and only after I was grown did YaYa explain to me how this came about.

Long before she became a Christian, she lost a son. Following Greek tradition, she mourned her loss by wearing nothing but black—black dress, black stockings, black shoes, black purse. After Grandma became a Christian, God spoke to her, *Stop* mourning. I am the Lord of *life,* not of death. Immediately, YaYa started to celebrate life by wearing bright colors. This attitude of celebration explains her positive influence in my life.

YaYa often heard from God and, like Mary in the Bible, she knew how to hold things in her heart. After I had grown up, she told me of two visions she had received about me. She liked to tell me the first vision about my birth because it assured her that I would live and that God would use my life.

YaYa's second vision occurred when I was still a boy. She saw me walk into the living room of her apartment. From the top of my head to the bottom of my feet I was covered with diamonds. And the light reflected the glitter of the diamonds, my whole body appeared as bright as the midday sun. The Lord spoke to her, *His talents will shine throughout the whole world, and he will influence many lives.*

YaYa told me about this vision when I was in my late teens. By then I already knew that my future ministry lay in my piano playing.

In reflecting on this, I'm reminded of YaYa's quiet wisdom. She waited until the appropriate time to tell me of her vision. Had she told me earlier, I might have taken it as a club to force me into serving God. Instead, she waited until God's call had already been confirmed in my heart.

My grandmother died in December 1977. And while I believe her vision and the interpretation, I also think God gave her a literal picture of something that would take place later in my life. She only lived to see my early television appearances with Kathryn Kuhlman, where I wore a variety of tuxedos. But I finally added sequins and what I call a dash of flash. Had Grandma lived, I think she would have seen me with such glitter that I certainly would have appeared to be covered with diamonds from head to toe.

Grandma was more than a woman who heard from God; she constantly wanted to tell others about God. As far as I'm concerned, my unschooled grandmother was one of the great orators of the faith because she talked so easily and eloquently about God to anyone. No matter where she went, YaYa carried a Greek New Testament in her purse. And though she couldn't read a single word, she had memorized many Bible verses.

Many times as a child, I watched her walk down the street and suddenly pause and say quietly, "Yes, Lord. Thank You, Lord." Without hesitating she would then walk up to a stranger, a Greek whom she had never seen before, and greet that person in their common language.

When the person responded (and the people always did), she would ask, "What's your name? I don't know you, do I?"

They would introduce themselves to each other and, inevitably, somewhere in the conversation, YaYa would say, "Jesus loves you." Regardless of how the stranger answered, my grandmother would pull the New Testament from her purse. "Please, let me share with you the good news from God. Here, I want you to read it for yourself."

YaYa would open the Bible, point out a verse, and quote it while the stranger read. I'm not sure how she did that, because she couldn't read. Yet she would perfectly quote the verses. And she didn't use just the same four or five verses. She always seemed to have the verses that fit that person's particular need.

Besides speaking to strangers in New York, Grandma went back to Crete on several occasions to visit her birthplace. She would tell her old friends and neighbors about Jesus Christ and pray for them. YaYa once prayed for a woman dying of cancer, and the next day, the woman was seen walking around the island, saying to whomever would listen, "God has healed me through 'the saint.'" The locals thereafter referred to her as Christina "the saint," the one with "the gift of healing."

I first heard the story of YaYa the saint when I was nine years old. And though I never called her that myself, from that time on, I never doubted that my beloved YaYa was a real saint!

Chapter 4

CLASSIC STEPS

I wish everybody could have known Sister Marie Brown. Some of my happiest memories of childhood go back to her and to Glad Tidings Tabernacle. Sister Brown and her husband, Robert, started Glad Tidings Tabernacle in Manhattan. After the death of her husband when I was three or four years old, she became our pastor. And I loved her.

Although she died many years ago, I can still visualize her seated in the large, ornate chair on the platform. She would hold an open Bible on her lap and pray silently or join in the singing. A bosomy, heavyset lady, she wore nothing but white. With her hair pulled back into a bun and glasses on her nose, she resembled some kind of storybook picture of a grandmother.

Typically, as soon as our family reached the church on Sunday mornings, I'd leave the others and race down the hallway toward my Sunday school classroom. At her office, I would pause. "Good morning, Sister Brown," I'd call if I saw her. And then I'd wait, knowing her next move.

"God bless you, Dino," Marie Brown would say with a warm smile and a voice deepened by years of preaching.

She'd talk with me for a minute or two and then say again, "God bless you." As she squeezed my shoulder, she would slip an opened roll of Lifesavers into my hand.

"Thank you, Sister Brown," I'd say with a grin and pop a candy into my mouth. I especially liked cherry, and though I never told her, I'd hope each week she'd give me that flavor. I would then pop the next two candies into my mouth. As always, after the third Lifesaver I'd find a nickel wedged inside.

Her eyes would glow as she watched me take out the nickel. "Thanks a lot," I'd say. And for the third time she would offer a blessing. One morning Sister Brown added, "And I know He will, Dino. God has something special for you." Then she walked on and eagerly greeted others as they made their way to the classrooms.

Sister Brown may have given all the kids Lifesavers; I don't know. I do know that the half-pack of nickel-loaded Lifesavers was just one of the ways she let me know how much she cared about me.

When I think about childhood and especially about Glad Tidings, I remember this woman who was a saint of God, even to a young boy like me growing up in Manhattan. Through those gifts and her encouragement and respect, Sister Brown let me know she cared about me and, consequently, she exerted a lot of influence over my life.

I can't say she treated me as her favorite, because she had the ability to make all of us young people in the church feel special. Frequently, she urged us to get involved, to be part of the church. And she backed up her exhortation by giving us opportunities. For instance, I remember how I got to play the piano for the first time in front of the entire congregation. Sister Brown said to the man in charge of music, "Get Dino up there to play. Give the boy a chance." I was then asked to play. So I sometimes say my first public appearance was at Glad Tidings Tabernacle when I was seven. And it happened because of her encouragement.

I felt wonderful when asked, and the thought occurred to me that I must be pretty good. I didn't think of myself as the best or greatest, only that if Sister Brown thought I was good enough to play for the whole church, I must be accomplished.

As I walked over to the piano, I heard her raspy voice, "Play for Jesus, Dino! Play for Jesus!"

I sat at the piano and threw my heart into "I'd Rather Have Jesus." I knew it was Sister Brown's favorite. And though I played for Jesus, I dedicated it to her.

I loved those growing-up years when our family's life centered around Glad Tidings Tabernacle. I received my spiritual foundation at Glad Tidings and had the experience of playing in front of people who loved and cared about me. This helped build my confidence in myself and in my ability to play.

By the time I was fifteen, I played the piano regularly at Glad Tidings. When the church formed a teen's gospel quartet called the Christian Keynotes, I joined the group. We built up a repertoire and began to sing for the church, at summer camp, and at any place that asked us. I sang baritone and played piano at the same time. Although it was a lot of fun, my heart wasn't totally into this form of service because I desired only one thing—to play piano.

When I played at Glad Tidings, I often paused to glance up at the balcony and realized that people were sitting there, waiting, wanting to hear a message of hope. Some of them were burdened with problems, and all of them needed help. *Oh, God,* I prayed silently, *use me to speak to them, to touch them in their need.* I didn't have the ability to speak with flowing words so I offered God my one talent and asked Him to use it to minister to hurting individuals.

As far back as I can remember, I have felt something unusual, supernatural, happen when I play the piano. When I sit in front of the keyboard, my hands take over. I play unconsciously; my fingers touch right chords; the arpeggios and the melodies flow. Even at a young age, I felt as though I were preaching through my music. At church, I played as if I were singing; I wanted people to feel the music, to experience the message of God's care.

Maybe it's temperamental of me, but when I play I want everybody's undivided attention. God has called me to communicate through the keyboard. I don't think of myself as just an entertainer or a performer. I don't want people simply to say, "Oh, Dino plays so well."

At family gatherings when I was growing up, Mom would sometimes say, "Dino, play something." While I wouldn't have thought of refusing, I never, even at home, enjoyed going to the piano just to entertain.

Yet I love walking out on stage and facing a huge audience, trying to captivate them with music. They're ready to hear me and, I like to think, are open to feel the mood and the intent of the music. Every time I give a concert, I face an exciting challenge. That's why I love doing what God has called me to do. People come into my concerts depressed, hurt, and discouraged, and God gives me an opportunity to bring joy into their lives.

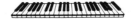

When I entered high school, I stopped taking lessons from Miss Smith. I grew tired of going through the same material again and again. And I felt she had nothing more to offer. She had given me a good foundation, and her ability as a teacher lay in that area. So I quit. Fortunately, we moved to the Bronx about that time, which helped me make the change because Miss Smith realized it wasn't convenient to travel into New York City every Saturday.

Not having Miss Smith meant that during high school I was on my own musically. I hardly ever played at school, preferring to play for the church and for youth groups. I graduated a semester early because I wanted to finish school and get busy in my life's work for God.

While I yearned to serve God, I had no career direction. When people asked me what I planned to do, I usually responded, "I want to play the piano." That's all I could say with certainty. As I prayed regularly for guidance and no answer came, life started to become a little foggy. "God, what do You want me to do with my music? Show me." Yet no door opened for me.

For a short time I considered becoming an architect like my Uncle Mike; but that idea didn't last long. As soon as I started making plans for training, I knew my heart wasn't into architecture or anything else except music.

After high school graduation, my sister, Chris, enrolled in Eastern Bible Institute (now called Valley Forge Bible College) in Pennsylvania. There she met her future husband, Paul Bartholomew. When he graduated, they married, and he enrolled at Central Bible College in Springfield, Missouri, to earn his master's degree in Bible. Since they were in Springfield when I graduated, I decided to try Bible College for a semester. I also wanted to learn more about the Bible and how to minister to people while I waited for God to direct me further.

While in Springfield I became a singer in the Revivaltime Choir, which had attained national recognition because of its records and the Revivaltime radio program. The Revivaltime Choir traveled many weekends, and though I enjoyed being on the road, I never realized that this would prepare me for my lifetime's work.

As strange as it may sound, I never played for the Revivaltime Choir because I wasn't good enough. Although I had learned to sight read, I couldn't read fast enough to keep up with the choir. God had given me a natural ability, yet as I watched the accompanists, I recognized that Dino still had a lot to learn.

More than once this lesson has become clear to me. Even today, I know I can always learn a little more and continue to improve.

Before the semester ended, I decided to go to a college where I could get help with my music—a Christian college that offered professional courses in music.

I'm going to concentrate on the piano, I vowed to myself. *I'm going to become a good pianist.*

I returned to New York and enrolled at The King's College in Briarcliff Manor, New York, where they offered the kind of music courses I needed.

I applied for and received a student loan to pay for most of my music courses. That eased part of the financial burden. But my parents still made sacrifices for me to go to college. Since The King's College is located forty-five minutes from New York City, I lived on campus. Mom worked double shifts as a waitress just to make that extra money for my expenses. I've always appreciated my folks' taking on the extra load for my schooling.

The first year the college required me to take general studies, but I also got what I really wanted—music theory and other basic music courses I lacked. Miss Smith had taught me how to play, but she seldom explained the reasons behind the writing or the playing. Yet, as much as those courses helped, I soon discovered they weren't enough. I needed more specialized training in piano technique and performance.

After weeks of agonizing I made another decision: I decided to apply for an audition at the prestigious Julliard School of Music in New York City. If accepted as a student, however, this would mean a further strain on my parent's finances. My parents gave no sign, however, that this would be difficult for them.

"We'll make out fine," Dad always said when I visited home. "You go ahead."

"You do what you feel God wants you to do," Mom said. "And you don't worry about the money. God will provide. He always does."

YaYa hugged me. "Dino, this is to make you better to serve God. Do it."

Encouraged by my family, I set up an appointment and auditioned for Leland Thompson, one of the teachers at Julliard. A redheaded, middle-aged woman, Leland had worked as the assistant to Madame Levine—Van Cliburn's teacher. She seemed to have little regard for the way she dressed, as if clothes were of minor consequence. For her, only music mattered.

For the audition, I played "His Eye is on the Sparrow," using my own arrangement, which I hoped would show her my talent. Leland sat and listened silently, expressionlessly.

"And what kind of music have you mostly been playing?" she asked when I finished.

"Church music. Gospel." Although many professionals looked down on gospel music, I wanted her to know the truth, so I explained about my experience playing in the church.

"Why do you want to study at Julliard?"

"I want to sharpen my ability to play gospel music. I don't think I'll get much better without understanding classical music and being able to play it well."

To my delight, I was accepted. I continued my work on a degree at The King's College and commuted to Julliard for piano lessons.

As I would learn, Leland had never been a great performer but she was an outstanding teacher. A highly intelligent woman, it showed not only in the way she spoke and in the questions she asked, but in the way she approached her instructions. She concentrated on the student as well as the music.

Leland Thompson accepted my musical orientation as it was, and never sneered at gospel music. As I learned from other students, some of the teachers said of gospel music, "That's garbage. You must learn to play *real* music," by which they meant classical. But Leland didn't function that way. She worked with me at my level and allowed me to choose the direction of my musical career.

We never discussed whether I would be a great musician—I'm sure she knew I would never turn out to be an outstanding classical pianist because my heart was too much into gospel music. She taught me as much as I could absorb. As a matter of fact, years later when I recorded one of my first albums, a big production album with Ralph Carmichael, Leland Thompson advised me on several things.

Although an excellent teacher, Leland practiced the teachings of Christian Science and used some of her mind-over-problems techniques on her students. "You can cure your own problems," she often said. "You can do anything you make up your mind to do. Think it through."

For her, every problem, every hindrance was in the mind, and sin was an illusion. She kept pushing me and her other students to free our minds "so that you can free yourselves."

While I never bought into her religious doctrines, and she never tried to change mine, Leland's constant barrage of Christian Science did help me as she impressed on me that a major step in getting free of any difficulty is first to identify exactly what troubles us instead of being tossed around with vague concerns and general worries. "God gives us minds and the ability to think through our problems," she said. "Identify the cause of the problem, eliminate it, and then you can become free."

Leland grasped the uptightness and frustration that resulted from my being brought up in a strict religious environment. When I first came to study at Julliard, I struggled like many young Christians with a variety of conflicts. While my family wasn't legalistic in the sense of constantly speaking against going places or enjoying life, many of our Christian friends were. They implied that we had no right to experience happiness or pleasure in this life; that only comes in the hereafter.

Leland had a way of making me look at a problem from several levels. She would talk about the mind and the need to understand myself before I could play perfectly. Sometimes she talked more like a psychiatrist than a music instructor because she kept probing into my background, commenting on my uptightness, asking questions about where I had come from and how I felt about music, about people, about life, about performing. She helped me recognize that when I was uptight about my values as a Christian, it showed in my performance. She kept probing, trying to help me find the cause of my strain.

When I began to tighten up as I played, Leland would ask such questions as, "Are you hearing this rhythmically? That must come first." Once convinced that I was, she would say, "Now, I want to be sure you grasp this harmonically. Do you?"

During this questioning she was trying to get me to talk about what was bothering me and to define it verbally. "Dino, it's inside of you," she said. "It's a process. Just keep trying to identify who you are."

I listened. Although I tried to understand, she wasn't getting through to me. But being the persistent woman she was, Leland Thompson kept on.

One summer evening I walked into Leland's studio for a lesson. I sat down in front of the keyboard and before I started to play, she explained her theory to me again. "Know yourself," she concluded and nodded for me to begin to play.

The way she explained the theory that day finally penetrated my mind (or maybe it had just taken a long time to soak in). I understood. I knew who I was, that I belonged at Julliard, learning to play better. I knew God had given me a special talent and was preparing me to use it.

Understanding Leland's instructions for the first time was like a powerful, emotional conversion experience when everything suddenly takes on meaning. The music had come alive inside of me; now it was ready to live through my fingers. I placed my hands on the keys and played the piece as if it were no challenge. Suddenly I wondered why this piece had given me so much trouble.

Although Leland said nothing while I played, I could sense the triumph she felt for me. I had broken into a new realm as a musician—and as a person.

I left that session feeling that from then on, I could handle any technical problem. And since that day, I've never had any serious problem playing new music.

Leland, like so many of the other women in my life—YaYa, Mom, Sister Brown, and Kathryn—exhibited one primary concern for me: to become the best I could be *no matter which direction it took me.* No matter what I would have chosen to do with the rest of my life, she, as well as the others, would have said, "Dino, if this is what you want, then I am behind you." Without question, this unconditional affirmation and support instilled in me the confidence and security I would later need to persevere in my pursuit of a career in music.

Chapter 5

FORWARD MOVES

Visions of being on a concert stage where Christians and non-Christians listened to my playing often filled my thoughts. I hadn't worked out how I would accomplish that. I didn't know of any Christian pianists who held concerts, though hundreds of singing groups toured the United States. Yet I had a dream and I couldn't let go. Slowly that dream changed into an unshakable conviction.

Just having that inner conviction gave me a sense of direction, and I knew that God was leading me forward. I spent my weekends at home and played at Glad Tidings. During the week I commuted from The King's College to Julliard to continue my piano lessons with Leland Thompson as well as to take other courses. The Julliard professors concentrated on technique and public performance—skills I needed to learn.

One day the Trumpet Trio from Houghton College came to The King's College looking for a piano player to replace their keyboard man. The Trumpet Trio featured Ron Kerr and Bob McKenzie, who later became head of the Benson

Publishing Company, one of the top record producers of gospel music.

After auditioning me, Ron Kerr said, "Yeah, you're what we want." That I could play by ear as well as read the notes was a combination they found fascinating. Few musicians do both with ease.

After a few weeks playing with the trio, they gave me a regular spot for a piano solo in their concerts. We did our traveling on weekends and came back in time to be in class Monday morning. I accompanied them for two years.

These men, who were professionals even then, taught me a lot and expected me to be thoroughly professional as well. By accompanying them, I got valuable preparation for my future ministry. I gained experience in performing before different audiences—people who didn't know and love me as the people at Glad Tidings did. I had to make it on my talent alone.

I recognized the next forward step in 1963, a few days after I had given my senior recital at The King's College. Dr. Robert Cook, the president of the college, called me into his office. "Dino, we've all been impressed by your musical ability."

I thanked him for his kind words. Then he mentioned the real reason for wanting to talk to me. "Dino, would you be interested in staying on at The King's College to teach? We need a good piano teacher, and we think you would be excellent."

Everyone already considered me one of the main pianists at The King's College. I suppose they thought I was advanced in my piano playing. I wasn't great, at least not by my own standards, and I still had so much more to learn. Yet the opportunity seemed right for me. I could teach and continue going to classes at Julliard. "Yes," I said, "I'd like doing that."

Teaching at The King's College turned out to be a fine opportunity for me. I graduated with a Bachelor of Science degree in 1963. All the while I had been studying hard, doing everything I knew to become a fine musician. I wasn't lazy about practice and put in as many hours as I could squeeze in, often neglecting social opportunities.

By going to classes at Julliard and doing the practicing demanded, I soon realized I was too busy. I had too many students and never seemed caught up on anything. Besides that, I wanted time for dating.

I had dated a few girls during my college years. And by 1963, I had gotten serious about Lojan, a pretty blonde student at The King's College. Initially, her looks and intelligence impressed me. As we got to know each other, she impressed me even more because she was a fine Christian, a straightforward, highly talented person. She also liked to sing. (Strangely enough, I recently realized that all of the women who appealed to me romantically liked to sing.)

Lojan and I became engaged. However, one significant factor hindered our relationship. She couldn't understand the close ties in my family. Her father worked with a foreign missions board and had frequently traveled, so each person in her family had been independent of the other. Consequently, she couldn't understand what it was like to come from a poor family that survived because of the strong relational bonds.

"Don't you have any private life?" Lojan asked several times. Or she would tell me what a fine family I had before adding, "But they're too Greek. Too clannish."

"That's the way we are. Family is important."

"Important, of course," she said, "but yours seem all-important." Another time she asked, "Can't you do anything without talking it over with your family? They seem to control your life." The anger in Lojan's voice made me wonder if she would ever grasp that not only our family but all the other Greek families we knew were close.

Although my parents would never have advised me not to marry her, I sensed that they didn't believe she was right for me. At the same time, they genuinely liked her.

We had been dating a couple of years before I began to feel that, aside from the family issue, she really wanted to marry someone with a theological background, like a pastor.

By the end of that year of teaching at The King's College, my big romance was falling apart and I wasn't sure what to do. Perhaps, I reasoned, if I could get away for a short time, we could both reassess our feelings and our relationship.

The perfect opportunity came when Leland Thompson told me of a unique opportunity to travel to Europe and study for the summer on a scholarship. This was open only to advanced pianists who were recommended by recognized teachers. To qualify for acceptance I needed to have a letter of recommendation from Leland Thompson. Leland wrote the letter and I was accepted. Again my folks had to scrape to help me with my expenses, this time to and from Europe.

When I start making money, I vowed, *I'm going to make it up to them.*

They never complained about the hardship. "We want the best for you, Dino," Mom often said.

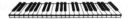

Despite the uncertainty of my relationship with Lojan, I could hardly wait to study at Fountainebleau Conservatory, outside Paris. I kept thinking, I'm this kid from Manhattan and I'm going to learn from the best in the business. And the best had to be Nadia Boulanger. Although now dead, she was at that time one of the most highly respected educators in the music world. Besides Boulanger, which would have been exciting enough, a number of outstanding musicians came to Fountainebleau to teach, including Arthur Rubenstein. I knew he'd be there, but I didn't know I would have the chance to talk to him and to study under him as well.

The curriculum included nothing but classical music with classes during the day and concerts at night. I loved everything. Although I felt out of my depth at times, the whole summer was stimulating and I gained so much. Most of the other students had been playing under the guidance of top-quality teachers since they were four or five years old. Those my age had received more musical instruction than I would ever have—and felt they were still not ready to make their mark in the world.

While studying at the Fountainebleau Conservatory during the summer of 1964, I realized I wasn't going to be a classical pianist. I didn't have the background, the training, nor the inclination. Not that such a career had been a serious option, yet with all the instruction I had received at Julliard, a few times I asked, "God, is this the way You want me to go?" Yet always I would ask, "Help me make the right choices."

I often laughed to myself while I was at Fountainebleau. To our family and friends at Glad Tidings Tabernacle, I had seemed precocious when I picked out the notes of a gospel song at age three. Yet that summer, I met students who told me they had played minuets by the time they were four years old. I didn't want to believe it.

In the midst of my euphoria, I began to receive letters from Lojan. Each letter conveyed a slight but definite shift in her feelings about me. After the fourth letter, Lojan candidly told me, "I have started dating another man. We're praying together." I read between the lines and knew I was losing her.

As her letters continued to arrive, each one told me more of the progress of their relationship. The other man was a student at The King's College and was preparing to enroll at Moody Bible Institute. I was crushed and confused. I had hoped this time apart would give us some answers, but these were not the answers I had hoped for.

Two weeks before my classes finished, I received the letter I had dreaded. She began: "I don't know how to tell you this, Dino, but . . ." After the first sentence, I skimmed through the rest of the four-page letter. He was the kind of man Lojan wanted; she loved him, and she knew it wouldn't work out between us.

As I crumpled the paper, I realized that I still cared deeply about her. My heart was broken, but I consoled myself thinking God had answered my parents' prayers.

Being away for two months prepared me to accept the inevitable breakup. Despite the pain from Lojan's letter and my awareness of being the least-trained student at Fountainebleau, I loved my time there. Both the staff and the atmosphere challenged me to work harder, the highlight being my opportunity to study under Arthur Rubenstein.

I returned to the United States humbled by the experience in France, yet feeling more self-assured. While all the students were extremely talented, many of them with greater ability than mine, that knowledge didn't depress me. I was good at what I did, and I knew I could be better.

There are finer pianists, but I'm committed to do the best with the talent God has given me. One thing I know I do well is start with a familiar melody, stay with it, and embellish it with chords. I stay with the melody because that's what communicates a message. I want the words of a familiar hymn or gospel song to be in the minds of the audience as I give those lyrics new life and meaning with my arrangements.

I'm not sure how this musical gift works, only that it does. This gift is more than natural ability, training, or technique. I think of it as God breathing His Spirit into what I play.

God uses an unreserved commitment, that yieldedness, to make a person's gift work. I believe that as I yielded myself and my talent to God, the Holy Spirit added uniqueness and influenced people and changed their lives.

Not only did I receive some of the best instruction ever, but just as important, I learned about my ability—and my limitations.

In fact, it would have been a perfect summer except for one thing: I received a letter from the federal government.

Chapter 6

IN THE ARMY?

"Greetings," began the official letter from President Lyndon Johnson, "You are hereby notified to report to Fort Dix on October 23, 1964. . . ." My eyes skimmed ahead and words like *Army* and *drafted* stuck out.

Me, in the Army? I asked myself as I read the draft notice again. *What will I do in the Army?* I wasn't athletic and had never been involved in sports or taken much interest in social activities. My whole world had revolved around church, music, and of course, piano. I'm patriotic and believe in this wonderful country; I couldn't see how my being drafted would be of any help in the undeclared war that had been going on in Vietnam since December 1961.

The military had been on my mind from time to time because our country still had a draft law. And like all good citizens, I had registered shortly after my eighteenth birthday. Yet I kept my life so filled with other things, I hadn't thought seriously about actually serving in the military. And now the government wanted me.

"What do I do now?" I asked myself aloud. I also asked Mom and Dad and YaYa. They didn't want me to go, of course, yet they also had strong patriotic feelings.

"We pray," YaYa said. "That's what we do. God knows." Then her eyes twinkled. "And God lead us."

"Dino, the Lord will show us," was all Dad said.

Mom watched the TV news, and I knew it was hard for her to release me, her only son. "Yes," she said slowly, "we'll pray for God to intervene. But more than that, we want the Lord's will to be done."

God didn't give me any specific guidance. I had already committed myself to teach for another year at The King's College. Surely, I reasoned, it couldn't be God's will for me to go into the military service. They needed me at the college.

For several days, I worried about going through basic training, about being sent to Vietnam, about fighting in a war that I didn't understand, and of course, about cutting my hair. Certainly, I thought, if I cut my hair I'd lose my strength to play the piano.

Dr. Cook and his staff understood my dilemma and confusion. They tried to get me an exemption because of my teaching at The King's College. The draft board ruled against the petition.

A week before I was to report for my physical examination for the army, a friend pointed out, "Dino, since you have to go into the army anyway, you could do better for yourself if you enlisted. You can enlist right up until the day you're supposed to report for your physical. Have you considered enlisting?"

"Are you crazy?" I asked. "If the army drafts me—and they will unless God intervenes—at least I'll only be in for two years. If I enlist, that's a *three-year* obligation!"

"Yes," he said, "but if you enlist, you get to make choices."

"Like what?"

"You can try out for special services."

"So what's that?" I asked, being completely ignorant of the military. "The army is still the army."

"True," he answered, "but by enlisting, you could audition for the army band. That's part of special services—the noncombatant jobs. Those in special services do things for those doing the fighting. If you're good enough—and I know you are—you stand a good chance of being assigned to play the piano for three years."

Once I got past the idea of serving three years instead of two, his advice sounded better and better. Wanting to be sure my friend knew what he had been talking about, I asked at the recruiting center. The recruiter assured me that I could play in the army band if I passed the audition.

"How do I audition?"

"That comes after you sign up," he said with a big smile.

"That way, if I don't pass, I'm caught anyway."

"If you're good, you won't need to worry," he said.

With some reluctance, on October 20, 1964, I signed away the next three years of my life. And I continued to worry. *I'm still liable to end up in Vietnam with an extra year to serve besides.* At that point, I prayed fervently, "Oh, Lord, what am I going to do over there?"

A few days later I auditioned for the First Army Band. To my relief, the officer-in-charge told me that after my six weeks of basic training, I would become part of the United States Army band. When I asked, however, he gave me no assurance where the army would send me. "Anywhere they need you," was all he finally said.

The fighting continued to build in Vietnam. The army was shipping just about everybody to Southeast Asia— even those in special services. Nightly updates on the television news reported unbelievable casualties.

A week later I began basic training at Fort Dix, New Jersey. Every new rumor (or scuttlebutt as we called it) that flew through the door, I listened to and accepted as fact until we learned the truth. Most of the rumors amounted to nothing, but I didn't learn that for a long time.

While Vietnam hadn't yet become the dividing issue in America, one news correspondent labeled it the "six o'clock war," because each night Americans could sit at their tables and watch our soldiers killing and being killed.

"You know," I overheard one sergeant say to another, "in a news conference, the Attorney General said we're going to stay in Southeast Asia even if it takes every fighting man we've got."

"Yeah," his friend answered and nodded our way. "Most of these poor guys here might as well figure on crawling through rice paddies."

As I walked away, I kept thinking of that conversation. *What if our company did go to Vietnam? What if they made me a combat soldier?* I'd have to go but I wouldn't like it. During basic training, worries about the future constantly came up. I suppose my faith had never been tested before, because I never seemed to have any peace over the matter. I prayed—a lot.

Regularly I wrote Mom and YaYa. Even though I knew they prayed faithfully every day, I urged them to pray. Several times I called home, and just hearing their voices made me feel better.

"God is with you," YaYa would say. "You can be at peace."

Mom would say comforting words as well. And for a day or two, I actually had real peace.

At the end of recruit training, I received my orders: I read past all the military jargon on the printed form until I came to the section typed in all caps: "YOU ARE HEREBY ASSIGNED TO THE FIRST ARMY BAND, FT. WADSWORTH, NEW YORK."

I started laughing, unable to believe what I read. After all my worries and frenzied prayers, I was being assigned as a pianist at Fort Wadsworth—right on Staten Island. While being part of the army, I'd be stationed in greater New York City. I could still attend church at Glad Tidings. And on top of that, I could go home at night to be with family and friends.

"Thank you, God," I said. "As long as I have to be in the army, this is the best thing you could possibly do for me."

In the band, we wore our dress blues on special occasions—most of the time we played publicly. We marched down Fifth Avenue on Memorial Day and again on the Fourth of July and on other holidays. Of course, I didn't play the piano, I played the glockenspiel (sometimes called the bell lyre), a percussion instrument with tuned metal bars in a frame, much like the piano except it is played with mallets.

God had set up a wonderful arrangement. By day I served the army, slept in my own bed at night, and spent most of my free time at Glad Tidings. At the church I became the music director and was in charge of the entire music program. The church had a large choir and some very talented singers. The church also staged a large Christmas production at Hunter College. In those days I thought of it as a big production, and, from my limited experience, it was.

What a wonderful time it was for me. I was doing what I loved best; I was serving my country, earning a little money, and thoroughly enjoying life.

For a year and a half, I lived almost as I had before going into the army. God had given me the perfect place to serve, and I testified of this to a number of my friends.

Then, after eighteen months and totally unexpectedly, I received startling news: The men in our company were going to be transferred.

Having no idea where the army would send us, we all listened to the rumors around us—there were always rumors about Vietnam and the latest figures of casualties on both sides. Vietnam, the war now building up with troops going over weekly, filled much of our conversation, and we constantly heard tales of brutality, the terrible treatment of American prisoners of war, and, above all, the high death tolls of American GIs.

One Tuesday morning we lined up in the orderly room where we received our daily orders. But today was different. And we all knew it. As each man heard his name called, he answered, stepped forward, and took the military form. Each man skimmed down to the words that said where he was going. Before my turn came I heard groaning around me and words like "'Nam." I was scared, just like most of the others, although none of us admitted it.

Then I read the important sentence: "YOU ARE HEREBY ORDERED TO REPORT TO THE TWENTY-FOURTH INFANTRY DIVISION IN AUSGBURG, WEST GERMANY . . ."

I didn't like being transferred, but it was a relief to read the word *Germany.*

America maintained many military installations in Europe, the largest number of troops being in West Germany. Since West Germany was the closest Western-allied nation to the Soviet bloc, American soldiers had served there as part of the peacekeeping forces since the end of World War II. Our government's policy was to provide a deterrent to the Soviets with our presence.

"Lucky bum," someone called me upon hearing of my orders.

"Yeah, I'd trade with him in a minute," said another.

I should have been overjoyed because the army was shipping most of the other guys I had served with directly to Vietnam. When I received my transfer in mid-1966, the still-undeclared war had heated up considerably. In America more voices clamored about the unjustness of our being in Southeast Asia.

Instead of being thankful that I didn't have to go to Vietnam, I got upset at God. "Why, Lord? Why are You uprooting me now? I'm halfway through my enlistment. Why are

You taking me out of this wonderful situation that You provided for me in the first place? Look at all I can do for Glad Tidings and still serve my country. I thought this was Your will for me to be here. It has been ideal. Perfect. This transfer doesn't make sense. Please stop this, God. You have to intervene somehow."

I tried to get out of being transferred to Germany. By going to see the personnel officer, I hoped I could have the orders rescinded.

After hearing my request, the lieutenant said, "Kartsonakis, you have been ordered to Germany. Those are your orders. Be thankful it's Germany and not 'Nam."

"Yes, sir," I said as my final word.

I had to go. The more I thought of how things had been, the more downhearted I became. No longer would I enjoy the soft duty of living at home, spending time with my neighborhood friends and serving God in my home church.

Rumors again filled the conversation on the base before I left. The one that troubled me the most was that once I arrived in Germany our band would join the troops in the field. We would stay with them, right at the edge of battle, helping to boost the troops' morale. I tried not to think of that happening.

I spent ten days' leave at home, saying good-bye to everyone. My parents and YaYa knew my keen disappointment. I don't recall that Dad said much, but I knew he was deeply concerned.

"God is going to take care of you," YaYa said frequently and in a variety of ways.

"You belong to God, Dino," Mom reminded me. "We're trusting Him to take care of you."

They were right. I wished I could be so confident.

My orders called for me to fly by commercial air from LaGuardia directly to Germany. My folks came with me to the airport to see me off. They were in high spirits, but I didn't say much. I was confused, unable to understand why this had happened.

Eight hours later and no clearer in my thinking, I arrived at Munich and then went by train to Augsburg. Within an hour after my arrival at the base, the supply sergeant handed me fatigues. *No more dress blues,* I thought grimly. *No more marching in parades down Fifth Avenue. This is the army now—the* real *army.* The day after I arrived I found myself with the field band, playing the glockenspiel while the guys were marching. Easy enough duty, but I was miserable. God had taken me from a perfect situation and thrown me to the back of the world. My MOS (Main Occupational Service) was still music, particularly the piano. I should have been thankful for being kept out of Vietnam; instead, I could only think of the disruption of my life. The more I thought about it, the more depressed I became.

"How could you let this happen to me, God? You know I want Your will and I want to serve You. But why here in Germany?"

God didn't answer and no peace filled my heart. I continued, through this tough time, asking God to intervene and get me out of there.

I had been spoiled by living at home. And from my perspective, life got worse. Now I saw what army life was really like. As a private first class I was assigned to a large barracks with hundreds of men in bunks—all in one room, something I hadn't had to put up with since boot camp. I wish I could say I made a quick adjustment but I didn't. While I did what they told me and never got into any trouble, I hated the army; I detested being in Germany; I despised my living conditions; and I prayed for God to help me to live through the next eighteen months.

One Tuesday evening I felt so miserable I didn't know what to do. Dejectedly I walked over to the recreation building and saw a piano in the corner. I sat down and started playing. I needed to give myself a little therapy. Other men may have been around but I didn't notice.

After a while, another private named Stryker came over and leaned on the piano. "Hey, you're good," he said. "Keep on playing."

I thanked him and kept on playing for my own enjoyment and to try to blot out my depression.

Wednesday morning at roll call my sergeant told me, "Report to Colonel Pfieffer's office. On the double."

"What did I do?" was my immediate reaction. I felt like I was being called to the principal's office in school.

"I don't know," he said. "But you'd better get over there—on the double, Kartsonakis!"

As I hustled to Colonel Pfieffer's office, I wondered if I had played too long in the recreation center. Had I been too loud?

"Kartsonakis, come in, come in," Colonel Pfieffer said. His friendliness puzzled me and I wondered why he had called me in, but I felt more at ease. He motioned for me to sit in a chair near his desk.

"Last night Pfc Stryker told me how well you played," the colonel said.

"Thank you, sir," I answered, still wondering what I had done wrong.

"He wasn't the only one. It seems you created quite a stir," he said. "That's why I called you in. Tomorrow afternoon the officers' wives are having their monthly tea. My wife is in charge of the entertainment as well as being the social chairman. She'd like you to play. That is, if you'd be interested." He was making it clear that it wasn't an order, and I could turn him down.

"I'd love to," I said, glad to do anything to get out of the rut of my regime, even if only for a few hours.

"You don't need to prepare anything fancy," he said. "Just background music while they're having their social time."

The next day I walked into the cavernous officers' recreation building that had been nicely decorated for the wives' tea. An old upright piano had been rolled into a dark corner. I sat down and began to play. Within minutes I had forgotten everyone and everything—I was having a quiet, peaceful time moving from one song to another. I was supposed to be playing for the ladies in the room, but I had retreated into my own world of music. Feeling as if I were having a private therapy session, it was the best time I had had since arriving in Germany. As I played, I kept thinking, *This sure beats being out in the field.* And I was having a good time, milking the melody lines from favorite popular pieces like the theme from *Dr. Zhivago* and selections from *The Sound of Music.*

After I had played for at least fifteen minutes, a dignified, middle-aged woman came over to the piano. "Hello," she said, "I'm Mrs. McCafray." She was the wife of the one-star (brigadier) general and commanding officer at Augsburg. "What's your name?"

"Pfc Dino Kartsonakis."

"How long have you been in Germany?"

"Just about a month," I said.

Question after question followed. As soon as I answered one she asked me for more information. In the back of my mind, I wondered, *Why are you checking me out? What's going on here?* But because she was the commanding officer's wife, I didn't dare ask.

Before moving away she did say, "I have thoroughly enjoyed your playing. Practically everyone here has told me how impressed they are with your ability."

The next day I received a notice to report to the general's office. For the first time since arriving in Germany, I sensed that God was doing something in my life. Only the day before I had still been crying out, "Lord, why am I here? You've got to get me out of this." Maybe He was listening after all.

"Sit down, Kartsonakis," General McCafray said informally.

That was certainly a hopeful sign and I obeyed, waiting to see what came next.

"My wife was quite impressed with your playing at the tea yesterday."

"Thank you, sir," I said. I liked the man immediately and listened as he talked about the importance of maintaining good morale and of music as a wonderful morale builder.

"Kartsonakis," he finally said. "Would you be interested in playing at the Officers' Club in Munich? Full-time?"

Instead of responding with the great enthusiasm I was feeling, I tried to remain calm. "Sir, if you want to transfer me, I'll be happy to agree." My voice was steady, but my heart raced and I wanted to shout.

"You'll be living at the Officers' Club," he said. "Moving to the Officers' Club means you get private quarters upstairs. Your responsibility involves being available for the afternoon teas that my wife and the other women sponsor. We frequently have special guests from Nuremberg—generals and their wives. When we do, my wife usually wants special music. We'd also expect you to play occasionally for the dinner and cocktail hours."

When I walked away, I was elated.

Chapter 7

EMERGENCY LEAVE

General McCafray made the transfer effective immediately. He ordered two Pfcs to come to my quarters to help
me pack my gear—quite an honor since I was still a Pfc
myself.

Upon my arrival in Munich I discovered that he meant I
would play in the dining room. The officers had a beautiful
dining room with a lovely atmosphere and a good grand
piano. I was assigned to work under the sergeant in charge
of the Officers' Club. The officers and wives also had evening dinners and wanted to start something new to help
them relax. And I was also to play dinner music for visiting
officials and their wives, as well as for an afternoon tea or a
luncheon just for the wives.

"God," I prayed, "I'm sorry about all my complaining."

Some of the other soldiers started calling me Golden
Fingers. I recall one lieutenant saying, "Hey, Golden Fingers, you've got it made! All the wives like you. Nobody
would dare transfer you now!"

I laughed—and I hoped they were right.

I loved my assignment in Munich. One night as I lay in
bed, I told God, "As long as I have to be in the army, You've
made this just about as good as it could be."

I didn't know it was going to get better yet.

To make the situation even more wonderful, a few weeks after my arrival, Mrs. McCafray asked, "Would you be interested in studying piano in Munich?"

She explained that the army had an allotment of money to use to improve their men in whatever field they were in. The army would pay all my expenses to study at the Munich Conservatory.

"I'd love to!" I said without even trying to hide my excitement this time.

What an opportunity God had provided for me. Suddenly I realized that I would never have had this chance in the States. Finally I could grasp the reasons for being sent to Germany. And I told God how sorry I was for all the grumbling and complaining I had done. It was one of many lessons I have had to learn on patience and in trusting God's timing instead of my own.

If I thought I had it good in New York, it was better in Germany. I had a light schedule of duty that provided me with time to do what I loved doing most—playing the piano. I went to Munich for my lessons where I studied piano at the Munich Conservatory under some of the world's finest instructors. If I was scheduled to play, of course, I couldn't go to my lessons, but those times were rare.

German teachers were very demanding about perfecting piano technique and the study of Mozart, whom they considered their major composer.

"God," I prayed almost every day, "thanks for sending me to Germany in spite of all my grumbling and complaining. You do know what's best for me, and I keep forgetting."

By the mid-1960s the relationship between the Americans and the Germans had deteriorated, and many voices were telling us to go home. The army decided to promote activities to play down the rupture. General McCafray set up a tour for me to play in the music houses which were quite popular throughout Germany. Located in the larger cities, these were public auditoriums with a hall where the top artists performed. I thoroughly enjoyed this opportunity to play for the civilians.

Later I toured with another army guy named Paul Pittman, who was in the infantry. Paul also had MOS as a pianist and was studying at the Munich Conservatory. On our own, we plugged into an agency called American Pianists and did four concerts together. We featured a lot of Mozart and a number of four-hand arrangements on one piano. The Germans loved it. Not only did Paul and I have a splendid time, but it was good public relations for America and the American Army.

The general loved what we were doing because it resulted in positive press reviews that made the Army look impressive. From back home, friends wrote that they had read about me in the newspapers as one of the American pianists who was getting a good response from the German public.

Every time I played, the people welcomed me. For as long as I remained in Germany, I continued to get additional invitations to play.

The military people supported Paul and me with tremendous enthusiasm. Because of my additional training and my unique opportunities, I was continuing to improve as a musician.

When I played at military bases, several soldiers would huddle around the piano with requests. Between sets, they asked questions such as, "Where are you from?" "What do you do in civilian life?"

Their questions gave me a chance to talk about my background and my gospel work. A few times I witnessed to them about Jesus Christ. Many knew I was a Christian. I didn't preach, and I was a very private person. But they saw that I was different—I didn't carouse, take drugs, or get into any of the wild life.

When I was through with my work at the Officers' Club, I would go up to my room and write letters or read.

I attended church on Sundays with Phil and Sharon Wilkins, an Assembly of God couple, who became my special friends. Phil, a Pfc assigned to Special Services, and Sharon frequently invited me to their house, which became a home away from home for me.

General and Mrs. McCafray also became friends and treated me almost like a member of their own family. Years later I received a letter from both the McCafrays and the Pfieffers. They had seen me on television and wanted me to know that they enjoyed hearing and seeing me play again, that they were proud of me, and were glad they had gotten to know me in Germany.

Then came sad news. One night while I was playing at the Officers' Club, I received a telephone call from my mother.

"Dino, your dad's in the hospital," she said. "He had a heart attack."

In shock, I asked, "How bad is it?"

"We're not sure, Dino. They called it a massive coronary . . ." Mom's voice broke several times, and I knew she was choking back tears.

"How's he feeling right now?"

"He's still in a lot of pain."

By then I was already preparing myself for the worst possible news as I asked again, "What do the doctors say? About . . . about his chances?"

"They think he's going to make it . . . but, oh, Dino, he looks so sick and he hurts so bad."

As I listened, I tried to picture my father in the hospital. Never a man to talk much, he and I had grown close after I grew up. I realized then how much I loved Dad. Tears filled my eyes and I mumbled something about how sorry I was.

"He's asking for you, Dino. Can you come home?"

"I'll find some way to get leave . . ."

"He talks about you all the time," Mom said. "He loves you and he's so proud of you."

"Please tell him I'm coming and that I love him," my voice broke. "Dad's always been there when I've needed him." And as we closed off the telephone call, I realized that I really wanted to be there now that he needed me.

Immediately after Mom's call, I went to General Mc-Cafray and explained what happened. "Sir, I'd like to go home to be with my dad. Is there any way I can go home?"

General McCafray, well aware of my busy playing schedule, didn't hesitate. He knew I was close to my family. "We'll take care of it," he said and told me to pack.

He arranged for me to fly out the next morning in one of the army's cargo flights that went directly to New York. They built a couple of seats for me and I sat, the only passenger, in the middle of the huge cargo.

I thought of all the wonderful ways God had provided for me, even to the point of providing my transportation to and from Germany. And though I had only one week at home to visit with Dad, I needed to be there with him to be assured of his improvement.

"Just keep playing for Jesus," he said.

For the first few days, I didn't know if Dad would pull through. He slept most of the day and was too weak to talk when he was awake. The doctors, though optimistic, never would say, "He's going to make it." Instead, simply they said, "He's responding."

Finally, Dad took a turn for the better. Surprised and pleased that I had gotten emergency leave, he and I were able to talk quietly as he rested. He wanted to hear about everything I was doing and all the opportunities I had to play.

Each day after that, I could see Dad's improvement. And daily we drew closer as we talked through those quiet hours. I was thankful to God for giving me such a fine father.

Only a year earlier I had grumbled and complained about my duty. Now my heart overflowed with thanksgiving.

Dad returned home from the hospital, and I returned to Germany. In Germany I could perform for the public as often as I could work it into my schedule. It wasn't hard to return to Germany because I had less than a year left to serve.

This, I thought, is the good life.

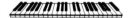

Six months before my date of discharge, General McCafray called me into his office, and we talked about my future. He had gotten excited about the response from the German public and the publicity for the army.

After he had talked a few minutes he said, "Now, here's why I've called you in. I've come up with an idea—something we haven't done before, but I think it's a unique opportunity for you. And for the army too, of course."

The general paused and stared at me, as if he wanted my answer. But I still had no idea what he meant, so I just listened.

"Dino," he said, "if you'll agree to extend your enlistment for one year, I'll arrange for you to travel all over Europe, play in every major city, and all your expenses will be paid. What do you think?"

"I'm flattered sir," I said, hardly able to believe what he was telling me.

"You'd be a kind of ambassador for the army. Spread good will and boost morale."

General McCafray had gotten so excited that before calling me in he had already presented the idea to headquarters. While they were receptive, he hadn't yet received a decision. Now he needed to find out if I would accept the offer.

As I listened, I was touched. After all, when my commanding officer and a man who had been a friend to me made such a kind offer, I hardly knew how to answer. Yet as he continued to talk, I realized that I didn't want to extend my enlistment.

Ordinarily I would have jumped at the chance. But deep within my heart, I felt that God was pulling me back home. An inner voice had been whispering for several weeks, *Something is going to happen in your life when you return to New York.* The message was so clear to me that I knew I couldn't extend my enlistment.

"Sir," I said, "I appreciate all that you've done for me. I'm flattered that you want me to be the army's ambassador, but I can't accept. I feel I need to go home."

"You're sure? No way you'll change your mind?"

"I've been praying about my future, sir," I said. "I believe the next step is for me to go back to New York."

"OK. I understand," he said, although I sensed his terrible disappointment. "I was afraid that might be the case." He thanked me for all I had done and for being a friend to his family.

Despite my speaking up, I experienced a certain amount of sadness in turning him down. He and his family often came to the Officers' Club in the evenings to hear me play. Over the months of my being stationed in Munich, I had gotten close to him and his wife as well as with other officers and their wives. It had been a nice relationship and I would miss them.

Perhaps it sounds strange for me to write about knowing that God was calling me back to the United States. At that point I had never played for any big Christian event. Other than concerts for the Army in Germany, my experience had been limited to playing at Glad Tidings Tabernacle and for the Trumpet Trio.

When I wrote to my parents and YaYa, they understood—as I knew they would. When I prayed, inside my head I could hear my grandmother's words, "God has something special for you to do, Dino."

This was one time I had no doubts. God was tugging at me. Something bigger and more meaningful than anything I had ever done before lay ahead. Although I had no idea what would happen, I knew it wouldn't begin until I was back in New York.

Chapter 8

THE DOOR OPENS

"How would you like an opportunity to serve the Lord? Playing?" Paul Dilena asked. "It's a great chance for you, Dino!"

I had been home exactly three hours on that October morning of 1967, when I received a phone call from Paul Dilena. An active member of Glad Tidings, Paul had taught my Sunday school class when I was in my teens and had always been a family friend. Paul is an outgoing, outspoken man, so he said with his usual enthusiasm, "I've been praying, and I think God has given me an idea for you!"

"I'm open, Paul," I said. "I know God has something for me; I'm just waiting for direction."

"Well, this might be it," Paul said. "How would you like to play for one of David Wilkerson's super rallies in California? He's doing these meetings once a month at Anaheim, at a place called Melodyland."

Before I had a chance to think it through, Paul started to sell me on the idea. "Pat Boone will be there and André Crouch will sing. Wilkerson's doing fantastic things through those big rallies."

I remembered David Wilkerson, a scrawny preacher from Pennsylvania. I first heard of him when he received unasked for but widespread publicity because of the trial of several members of a young gang called the Dragons. David didn't know any of them personally, only that they had brutalized, attacked, and killed a polio victim in the Highbridge Park section of Manhattan.

At the end of their trial in February 1958, David tried to speak with the judge in the courtroom on behalf of the gang members. Uniformed guards, thinking he was trying to attack the judge, grabbed David. As soon as he was released, a photographer asked David to hold up his Bible if he wasn't ashamed of it. Just as he complied, the man snapped his picture, which went out over the news services that day.

From that story, people all over the country heard about him. By the summer of 1958, David had moved to New York City where he formed a ministry called Teen Challenge to preach about Jesus Christ. Gang members, delinquents, and drugs addicts immediately responded to him, and he developed an outstanding ministry. In 1963, David wrote his story in a book called *The Cross and the Switchblade.*

I vividly remembered David Wilkerson coming to our church in the summer of 1958, though I was still in my teens at the time. The folks at Glad Tidings Tabernacle helped launch Teen Challenge—the first such nationwide, Christian-oriented effort.

"So, how about it, Dino?" Paul asked, still waiting for my answer. "Would you like to go to Melodyland and play for David?"

"I'm interested in playing someplace," I said. "A place where I can feel it's a ministry for God."

"Well, Dino, as soon as your folks told me you were coming home, I began to pray about this idea. I kept asking God to lead me, and I'm asking you now because this feels right."

"I'd love it," I said. "This could be an opportunity to play for God and to use my talent in a spiritual way. Maybe this is the reason God wanted me to come back to New York."

Wilkerson was in New York at the time. He didn't like to fly, so I agreed to drive with him to the West Coast. That presented no problem for me. We had plenty of time in the car to get to know each other better. It was a good time for both of us. The trip also gave me a chance to see parts of the western United States I had never before seen.

After we reached southern California, I played for the Wilkerson rally. I especially enjoyed the experience of seeing so many young people respond to the gospel.

Once in California, I decided to stay there. That was long before I'd heard of Nashville. And I expected more opportunities to be available to me if I stayed. The big rallies and gospel meetings were headquartered on the West Coast. Ralph Carmichael, one of the big names in Christian music, lived in California along with just about all the other talent I knew about in the Christian recording business.

After that first meeting, David occasionally asked me to play piano as a soloist in his meetings, but it was never a steady thing. For over a year, David helped me all he could. He even invited me to go with him and play in various cities in the United States. His audience primarily responded to the singers with youth appeal. At those rallies, André Crouch was usually the star of the music program.

While I enjoyed working with David and appreciated the opportunity, he and I had a different focus. He concentrated on reaching teenagers, especially drug addicts and youth from the ghetto. But I saw myself appealing to a middle-class audience.

I think David put me in the program out of loyalty to Paul Dilena (although he never said so) because the two men were friends. Paul loved me and my family and wanted to promote me, but he didn't have the contacts that I needed.

I was just getting started and enough money came in so that I could pay my bills. During those slow months I never lost the assurance of something big getting ready to happen to me. I kept praying for God to open the right doors and to close the wrong ones. As the days dragged into months, I got impatient. Because I felt God wanted me to stay on the West Coast, I remained in California—praying, waiting, and expecting some kind of break.

One night, early in 1969, a woman came up to me as I finished playing for the David Wilkerson meeting.

"You're good," she said.

I smiled, glad that she had liked my playing. Many times people would come up to express appreciation.

"My name's Ruth Martin," she said and then talked more about my playing. "You're not only good but you're too good for these meetings."

I felt my face flush; I knew what she meant.

"You really need to be with someone who can give you a chance to show your talent," she persisted, "a place to spotlight your marvelous playing."

"I've been in Los Angeles over a year now," I said, "and I'm just one of hundreds of guys looking for that kind of break."

Her shrewd eyes were taking me in, as if measuring me carefully. "Ever heard of Kathryn Kuhlman?" she asked.

I shook my head. "I don't think so."

"She's someone you need to know." By then I realized Ruth Martin was no ordinary fan. She was a bottom-line, assertive woman. She asked two or three more questions about what I was doing, what training and experience I had, and then asked, "How would you like to play for a woman who has a national ministry? She's on television and is in demand all over the United States."

"I'd sure be interested in talking to her," I said, trying not to let my enthusiasm show.

"Her name's Kathryn Kuhlman, and she could do a lot for your career."

I had been waiting for a break but this seemed too good to be true. We talked a few more minutes, and I tried to figure out if she was legitimate.

"What's your telephone number?" Ruth asked, writing it down as I gave it to her. "You'll be hearing from us." And then she was gone.

I had heard stories like this before. Some of them turned out to be great opportunities. Others came to nothing. For the next two days my emotions rode a roller coaster—one minute soaring with excitement and the next, plummeting to despair. Each hour with no telephone call brought increasing doubt.

By late the second day, I decided nothing was going to happen, so I visited the Paul Webb Agency on Sunset Boulevard. The Webb Agency handled the television accounts of the biggest names in the gospel world of the 1970s, including Rex and Maud Aimee Humbard and Oral Roberts. Webb also handled Kathryn Kuhlman.

Paul Webb had listed me with his booking agency, which meant I was to be available whenever someone called for a pianist. I went by Paul's office that day, as I did every few days, looking for a last-minute fill-in or a one-night job. They had nothing for me.

As I left the office and walked down the hallway, I saw Ruth Martin and a tall, thin, red-headed woman. Ruth's friend looked like a 1930s fashion model: She was about five-foot-eight, and her hair was parted in the middle and curled by finger waves.

"Dino!" Ruth called out and turned to her companion. "This is the Dino I was telling you about." Ruth rushed toward me as if we had known each other for years. Although she didn't think to introduce me to her companion, I had already figured out that this was Kathryn Kuhlman. "So you're Dino." Kathryn dragged out the three words so that they sounded like ten.

Who is this lady? Her raspy voice and dramatic gestures and movements increased her intrigue. Kathryn lifted her arm, pointed her finger at me and, as if some divine truth had suddenly been revealed to her, repeated, "You're Dino."

"Yes, I am," I replied.

"I've heard about you. I've heard good things."

Before I had a chance to respond, she stepped closer and started to question me. Surprisingly, she didn't ask about my experience, my talent, my training—just about my family. Obviously, Kathryn highly valued family.

"Where are you from?" she asked. "Are your parents still living? Are you close to your family? Do you miss them, being out here on the West Coast?"

We talked for several minutes and then she abruptly ended our conversation after I answered her final question. She just said, "It was very nice meeting you."

I told her the same and left. As I headed home, I wondered about all of the grilling; it didn't make sense.

Early the next morning Ruth Martin called me. "Dino," she said, "Kathryn liked you."

"You really think so?" I was shocked.

"No question about it, Dino. She liked you very much."

"I'm glad," I said, wondering if Kathryn Kuhlman was for real. I had never met anybody like her.

"If you'd like to play, come to the CBS studios next week. You know where it is? On Fairfax?"

"Yes, I know."

"Kathryn's taping shows and we'd like you for one show. Only one, but it could be a real opportunity. Dino, remember, if Kathryn likes you, she can open all kinds of doors for you."

After Ruth's call, I felt elated. I had made the big time. I phoned my parents in New York. They didn't know who Kathryn Kuhlman was, but they were happy because they knew I felt good about playing for her.

On an impulse I rented a tuxedo to wear for the telecast. When I arrived at the studio, Kathryn greeted me enthusiastically, "Oh, Dino, perfect. I love the tuxedo. Oh, just right. Just exactly right."

I then had a chance to see the genius of the woman in action. Kathryn directed first-class productions, and I was impressed. And to create the perfect image, she insisted that the propmen hang a chandelier over the grand piano, with a large floral arrangement behind me. Frankly, I thought it was quite outrageous. But it created a splendid effect.

At the appropriate time in the rehearsal, I played a beautiful and dramatic John Petersen number, "No Greater Love."

"Oh, Dino," Kathryn exclaimed. "That's wonderful! Truly wonderful. We're going to shoot it now." We did the whole number in one take, and I didn't make any mistakes.

Instead of leaving afterward, I decided to sit on the sidelines and watch her preach. Kathryn mesmerized me. She generated a genuineness and a presence that won me over and filled the studio. No one fidgeted. Even studio people who hovered behind the cameras stood transfixed.

I've never seen or heard anyone like this woman before, I thought.

After taping the half-hour program, Kathryn came over to where I was sitting. "Dino, I like your playing. You are so wonderful! So gifted. Dino, we tape three shows a day. I know I didn't ask you in advance, but would you play for the next two shows? You are so magnificent."

"Of . . . of course," I stammered, hardly able to comprehend what was happening. I didn't know how much of

Kathryn's praise to accept, but she obviously liked me. And I was eager to pursue the opportunity.

My talent opened the door to our friendship. I was young, so I could help draw a younger crowd to her show. That was part of Kathryn's genius—she knew exactly what to do and the kind of people to have on her program.

I played for two more shows—"How Great Thou Art" and "The Holy City"—and Kathryn and I talked more about my family between tapings. I've always been proud of my family. And coming from a Greek heritage where we place a lot of emphasis on family, I found it easy to tell her about all of us, including my wonderful grandmother, YaYa. From the first time we met, she seemed to value—even envy—my relationship with my family.

Kathryn's eyes glistened as I talked, and from time to time she would softly interject, "Oh, Dino, that is so marvelous." Because I'd never known families to relate any differently, it didn't occur to me to ask Kathryn about her family—if she ever felt alone or if she had the emotional support of a family.

By the time I left the CBS studio, I knew Kathryn and I had connected. God sent me to California, and I had waited for the right door to open. Even though Kathryn never once hinted she would use me again, I knew she would. I've always been a committed person, throwing myself into whatever I do. And from that day, I became a loyal supporter of Kathryn Kuhlman's ministry.

When Kathryn did call, I was there, ready to play. I played for three of her next nine shows. Then she asked me to come back for the next series. I had a large and varied repertoire, so I could play new music for every show. And having been raised on gospel music, I could play anything she requested.

Soon Kathryn wanted me as a regular. People began to expect special music from me, and they liked what they heard. I was feeling wonderful, and my family was happy because they watched me on a regular television show.

Almost from the beginning I considered Kathryn more than an employer; she was my friend. She had, in a sense, adopted me as part of her family. I didn't object because my own family lived three thousand miles away. And I missed them. Until my move to California, my life centered primarily around my family and Glad Tidings Tabernacle. I never lacked for someone to encourage me in my faith or my musical talent. Mom and YaYa, especially, had always been there for me. Whenever I faced a serious problem or felt confused on making a major decision, I turned to Mom and to YaYa.

So Kathryn's influence wasn't threatening—at first. Instead I welcomed her direction for my career. And we became friends.

Although I admired many things about her, I saw immediately that Kathryn had a unique ability in knowing how to make the most of any talent, including her own. Beginning with that first show, she created my image, every step of the way. She staged me and made me appear to be all glitz and glitter.

Each show, Kathryn stood at center stage and introduced me as if she were heralding the return of some great prophet: "Here's Dino, the greatest keyboard artist in the world!" Without saying a word, I would begin to play, the incandescent chandelier providing the perfect balance between shadow and light, projecting an atmosphere of intimacy to the scene, as well as an atmosphere of both drama and glamour.

Kathryn helped make me more than a keyboard artist. She possessed an unapproachable mystique and helped establish the same aura about me. I couldn't have anticipated the powerful control Kathryn would one day exert in my life.

Chapter 9

THE INNER CIRCLE

"Is this an orange?" Comedienne Ruth Buzzi, making the last word sound as if it contained seven syllables, pointed to the piece of fruit. "Oh, yessssss! It *is* an orange. A beautiful, divinely-shaped orange!"

On one of the top television shows of the era, "Rowan and Martin's Laugh-In," Ruth Buzzi imitated Kathryn (without using her name) as one of her weekly sketches. This particular scene showed Ruth/Kathryn in a supermarket checkout line. Wearing a red wig and a green silk gown with flowing sleeves, she touched each item of fruit, and with exaggerated gestures, extolled the orange's virtues, making it sound as if she had just discovered nutrition.

For weeks, Kathryn became the focus of Ruth Buzzi's good-humored skits. The audiences loved it, even those who didn't know anything about the real Kathryn.

For many people, Kathryn Kuhlman was a novelty, especially in being identified as a faith healer. Not only Ruth Buzzi (although she was unquestionably the best) but other television personalities loved imitating her.

When Kathryn heard about the Ruth Buzzi act, she invited me to her house. "Oh, Dino, everyone says it's so much fun." Naturally I'd heard about the Ruth Buzzi skits too, so I wanted to see it. Kathryn, Ruth Martin, and I watched the program together. Ms. Buzzi did a wild take-off, overemphasizing Kathryn's already melodramatic gestures and slow, carefully enunciated words. Kathryn laughed as she watched.

Immediately after the program, she wired Ruth a dozen roses. And in the enclosed note, she told Buzzi how flattered she was.

I liked that quality about Kathryn—she could laugh at herself. She wasn't insecure when it came to what people said about her because she knew who she was. She was also secure enough that she didn't try to change in the face of unkind critics' ridicule.

Kathryn never tried to be anything other than herself, which made a lasting impression on me. Some people can't believe that she lived like the rest of us. She enjoyed life and knew how to relax and have fun. She ate in first-class restaurants and shopped in stores that sold quality goods. She especially liked to travel and to shop in different countries. When in New York, Kathryn went to see Broadway shows—good, wholesome shows like *South Pacific* or *The Sound of Music.*

From my own upbringing in the church, I had the impression that sincere Christians didn't have time to unwind. Yet by observing Kathryn at work and at play, I saw the importance of balance in my life.

When Kathryn worked, she gave of herself unstintingly. And it showed. She created an incredible impact on audiences. God had uniquely gifted her, and I believe she was as sincere and committed as any Christian I've ever met. When Kathryn taped for television, she operated on a fully professional level and nobody worked harder than she did.

At CBS, celebrities, like Glen Campbell, snuck onto the set. "I just wanted to see what you're like," he said when he appeared behind the scenes. He was impressed with what a genuine person she was.

The headliners for the then-popular variety show, "Sonny and Cher," were televising on the same days. Once I spotted them in the hallway. Minutes later, they dropped over to meet Kathryn.

"You're the best," Sonny Bono said as he left. "We laugh but we know you're real."

On one occasion Carol Burnett visited her on the set. I'm not sure if they filmed it, but she did a surprise walk-on. "I think this woman is incredible! Every time I hear her, I feel I'm a better person!" The applause from the film crew showed that they loved it—and so did Kathryn.

As I watched the crew, it was obvious that they went beyond doing their regular jobs, always wanting to do something a little extra for her. Even the top people at CBS treated her with an awesome respect, and Kathryn, in turn, treated them kindly—everyone from Dick Ross (her producer) to the cameramen and the lighting crew.

CBS gave Kathryn the star treatment with her own dressing room, wardrobe woman, and makeup person. Mr. Cappleman, then head of the studio, respected Kathryn. It showed by the way he spoke to her. I particularly remember that after she had taped a hundred shows he had a huge cake brought in for a celebration.

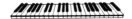

I started working regularly (almost exclusively) for Kathryn. She and I often talked for long periods between

tapings or while traveling. Frequently Kathryn invited me
out to dinner after the show. As Kathryn got to know me, I
became her loyal friend. Kathryn was quite a private person and didn't open herself easily to others. Yet before long
I became a member of an inner circle—the few people she
trusted and who had access to her.

Maggie Hartner, Kathryn's longtime secretary who lived
and worked mostly in Pittsburgh, was her most trusted
friend. They had met in the early 1940s, when Maggie was
working for the telephone company in Pittsburgh. The two
women stayed in contact and in the early 1950s, Maggie
quit her job and went to work for Kathryn.

The other significant person in Kathryn's life was Ruth
Martin. Ruth was a sharp lady who dressed in the best of
clothes. When we met at the David Wilkerson Crusade, she
was in her late thirties. Light-complexioned and blonde,
Ruth bubbled effervescently. Her quick wit, fast moving,
and rapid talking enabled her to step into just about any
situation and take charge. She loved moving around among
people, meeting with producers and cameramen, and she
somehow managed to keep things flowing. Through the
Martin Agency, Ruth handled the syndication of Kathryn's
television programs. Ruth's agency distributed the show,
and she made good money for her effort.

Over a period of months, Kathryn told me things she
hadn't shared with many people—if any. For instance, as
far as I know, I'm one of the few to whom she talked about
Eve Conley. I remember one night when Maggie Hartner
and I were her only dinner guests at her home. Maggie had
gone into another room. "This china is beautiful," I said
when I noticed the delicate patterns.

With a faraway look in her eyes, Kathryn said, "Eve Conley taught me about setting a table." I had never heard
Kathryn mention Eve, but I didn't say anything because I
assumed Eve was somebody I was supposed to know.

Kathryn touched the neat row of three forks and said, "I would never have known how to set these if it hadn't been for Eve. She taught me so much. She is more responsible for who I am today than any other friend I've ever had. She's gone now, but I still owe dear Eve so much."

"I wish I had known her," I said.

"Oh, Dino, I wish you could have known her, because you would have loved her too." Kathryn, in a rare nostalgic mood, told me that when they met in Pittsburgh in 1946, Eve was in her fifties and the widow of a wealthy, steel magnate. A woman of strong personality and aristocratic bearing, Eve wore nothing but black adorned with diamonds.

They met because Eve became fascinated by stories about this unusual woman evangelist who showed up in Pittsburgh and made such an impact on the community. Eve attended one of the miracle services at the First Presbyterian Church and introduced herself. "I was drawn to her," Kathryn said, "as if God had brought us together for that moment in life."

Immediately, Eve became Kathryn's best friend, a place no other person ever occupied. I don't know much about Eve's background (other than her being a wealthy widow), but she apparently had a wide range of talents, an innate understanding of people, and highly-developed organizational skills.

"Eve taught me about the world," Kathryn said. "The good part of the world. You know, things like the theater, how to dress, how to wear clothes to my advantage, selecting and wearing jewelry, as well as a number of excellent lessons on appreciating the finer things of life."

Over the years I worked for Kathryn, she would occasionally bring up Eve's name and tell me a little more about their relationship. One time she said, "Dino, Eve Conley was the best friend I ever had. But she was more. She was my . . ." she paused trying to find just the right word, "my mentor."

Eve Conley didn't stop with teaching her pupil about the finer things of life but moved right into the realm of Kathryn's ministry as well, actually training Kathryn's people— all of them, including ushers. Eve would explain, "This is what you do when babies cry . . ." In just about every phase of Kathryn's life and ministry, Eve was her teacher.

Then tragedy. One day Kathryn walked into Eve's house and discovered her friend's body on the floor. She had dropped dead, apparently from a heart attack. The person she most admired—and her best friend—was gone.

"It was one of the most heartbreaking experiences in my life," she said, her eyes brimming with tears. "Even after all these years I still miss her friendship."

Eve had taught her protégée well. Kathryn absorbed it all. Sometimes people called Kathryn "too demanding" when she insisted that everything be perfect. She learned her style and polish from Eve and put it to practical use.

Although I never saw a picture of Eve, Kathryn spoke of her often enough that I felt I had known the woman too. Kathryn never said, "I haven't told anyone else about my deep friendship with Eve," but she gave me the impression that she didn't talk about it to anyone else.

When she'd talk about Eve, I could hear the loneliness in her voice. Sharing those memories made me feel honored that she would trust me. Knowing about Eve also helped me better understand how this gifted woman had turned out to be a cultured person when she had had little formal training.

Kathryn never forgot the lessons Eve taught. At the Shrine Auditorium, Kathryn held meetings with the two hundred ushers, whom she herself carefully instructed. She wouldn't tolerate laziness or excuses and wouldn't keep employees who couldn't do their jobs the way she expected. One time a man showed up to usher but he wore scuffed shoes. Kathryn said to him, "You cannot serve tonight. We put forth our best, our very best, for Jesus. This isn't your best."

Yes, Kathryn, I thought, *Eve would be proud of you.*

I also felt sorry for Kathryn at times. She was famous and greatly used by God, but she had few people close to her. As I reflected on this, I thought how fortunate I was to have strong family support and to always have friends. Yet for much of her life, Kathryn's only close friends seemed those of us who were part of the inner circle.

Perhaps that loneliness motivated her to think of my family as a substitute. I only know that slowly Kathryn moved into my family circle. For a long time I was glad to see that happening because I had discovered she wasn't close to her own sisters who were the only family she had still living. In a number of ways, she became involved not only with me but with Mom and Dad and especially YaYa.

Because of being raised in poverty (although I didn't know it), I had one dream for my parents—that one day they would own their own home. Because of the outlandish price of houses in New York City, they never considered buying one.

One afternoon after I had worked with Kathryn for nearly three years, I drove her to Newport Beach. As we passed through Huntington Beach, we saw a number of small houses being built. I commented, "You know, some day I'd like to see my mom and dad have a house like one of those."

"Pull over, Dino," she said. "Let's look at them."

Surprised, I laughed. "Sure, why not?" I asked.

Kathryn jumped out of the car and went up to a completed model and scrutinized it, acting as if she were examining it as a prospective buy. She pointed out several nice features. As we talked we started calling it the yellow house because inside everything was yellow, including bright yellow carpet. There were large windows that allowed plenty of light inside and three moderately-sized bedrooms.

"Mom and Dad would love this," I said, not seriously considering the possibility of buying.

"Buy one of these houses for them," Kathryn said.

"Are you kidding?" I asked incredulously.

"Oh, Dino, why not?"

"I . . . I don't know . . ."

"You said it was your dream, didn't you?"

"Why don't we talk to the builder," I said, too overwhelmed to make a decision that quickly.

The builder wanted $27,500 for any of the yet-unfinished houses. To me, that was a lot of money. I kept hesitating, wanting to do something for them, but I'd never made any big investment like that before.

"Dino," she said, after we'd looked the place over again and both agreed that the builder asked a fair price, "Why don't you buy it for them?"

"I'm not sure," I hedged, thinking of the debt that I would incur and yet really wanting to buy.

"I think you should."

Her words shocked me, and I started telling her why I couldn't. "I'm not settled yet. Who knows where I'll be living two years from now? Probably the bank wouldn't give me a loan anyway. And what about making those monthly payments? What if I couldn't follow through?"

Kathryn laughed at all the reasons. "God can help you work it out. You'd like them to move out to California, wouldn't you?"

"Of course." I had often thought that I'd enjoy having my parents closer to me. The climate would certainly benefit my father, who had already gone through one serious heart attack and had developed other physical problems. New York City is a tough place to live if you don't have money. I figured that if I could bring Dad out to California it might extend his life.

"Make up your mind and trust God," Kathryn urged.

To make the purchase would be a huge step of faith for me. But Kathryn had been saying for a long time that if I really wanted something, I'd have to learn to take big risks. But I kept asking myself if I was ready for such a big step.

Again we talked with the contractor who happened to be on the job. "Tell you what," he said, "give me one hundred dollars and we'll work out a contract with you."

"I'll take it," I told the builder.

"I'm going to take that step of faith," I said to Kathryn, and then added, "But you'll have to loan me enough for the down payment because I don't have that much money with me."

Kathryn wrote out a check for one hundred dollars, which I repaid that afternoon.

Once I made the decision, I grew excited that I could finally buy a nice house for Mom and Dad. I could do something for them to let them know how I appreciated their years of sacrifice for me. I decided not to tell them about the yellow house until I had everything worked out with a bank and the house finished and ready for them to move in.

Kathryn had a delightful sense of humor, and she particularly liked to pull surprises in her meetings at the Shrine Auditorium. My buying the house gave her such an opportunity.

At our next meeting in Los Angeles, she introduced me by saying, "Now here's Dino, the man you've been listening to week after week." And, as only Kathryn could do, she raved about my talent. All the time, I remained seated at the piano, ready to start. But Kathryn wasn't finished.

"And," she said, her arms raised in mid-air, creating suspense, "now a surprise for Dino! His mother and father are

here tonight. They have just flown in from New York City for a surprise visit!"

The audience burst into applause, and my folks walked out onto the stage. The clapping continued as the audience gave my parents a standing ovation. Kathryn, still not finished, motioned for my parents to come forward. "Mrs. Kartsonakis, won't you say a few words to these wonderful people here tonight?"

"I'm always ready to speak for Jesus Christ," she said and the crowd cheered.

Mom showed real poise for a woman who wasn't used to speaking to five thousand people. After thanking Kathryn for flying them out to Los Angeles, she said, "We're proud of our son because he loves the Lord. And the fact that he's here tonight is a miracle!" Mom gave a dynamic testimony about God's work in her life and in mine.

My parents explained to me later that Kathryn had secretly arranged for them to fly to California at her expense. Although they would be moving out there a few months later, Kathryn wanted me to *show* them the surprise instead of just *telling* them about it. One more generous act on her part. Her generosity touched me deeply, and afterward I told her how much it meant to me.

The next day Kathryn and I drove Mom and Dad to see the house. We still had not told them about it. I wonder if anyone can imagine the thrill I received when I drove my parents right up to the front of the yellow house.

"Let me show you something," I said when we pulled up. My parents got out of the car and I said, "Mom, Dad, here's your house. Or it will be in a few months when they finish it."

"What do you mean, *our* house?" Mom asked, but even as she asked, the truth was breaking through to her.

"It's yours. You and Dad are going to live here, and YaYa can visit when she wants." (I had enough sense to realize that YaYa would never leave her fifth-floor apartment, let alone move out of New York.)

Several months lapsed before the house was ready for occupancy. But once finished, my parents left New York. From the time they moved to California, until my marriage, I lived with my parents in the yellow house. And when I later reflected on the events that followed and the anguish I endured, I was glad I could be near my family for support.

Chapter 10

TWO SIDES OF REALITY

For a few seconds, Kathryn paused in silent prayer. Then, a smile filled her face and she raised her arms. "There is a woman here who has had a severe heart condition for eighteen years," she announced. "God wants to heal her right now."

"Me! That's me!" cried out a middle-aged woman, as she pushed her way out of her row and raced forward.

As usual, Kathryn stood at the center of the stage. She had finished preaching, and one by one, she was calling people forward who had specific diseases. Hundreds of times, I had seen Kathryn Kuhlman in action, and I never got bored. Kathryn poured out her life and energy; she gave the audience everything she had. Within seconds a crowd of people would stream forward. Kathryn never touched anyone and never claimed to heal anyone.

Several helpers—of which I was one—stood at the edge of the platform. We didn't let anybody come on stage unless they claimed they had been healed. But as soon as someone told us they had been healed, we'd take that person to Kathryn.

Kathryn insisted before every service that she only wanted people on stage who had testimonies of healing.

On one occasion at the Shrine Auditorium, a woman slipped around the other ushers and moved past me. I caught a glimpse of her, aware only that she had an immense goiter on her neck. Kathryn couldn't have seen her because too many people blocked her view.

Before I had a chance to go over to the woman, Kathryn announced, "There's someone here being healed of a goiter. Right now. This very minute!"

Just then I grabbed the woman's arm, trying to stop her from moving toward Kathryn. At that instant I heard a loud popping and cracking like the breaking of egg shells. I watched that woman's goiter dissolve! In seconds, it was completely gone.

Kathryn Kuhlman had a special kind of sync with the Holy Spirit. In a service, Kathryn's pacing was perfect, ranging from her timing and her movements to her personality that captivated people when she walked out on stage. Even those who came to scoff found themselves caught up in the fervor and the electricity that emanated from her charisma.

Over the months as I watched Kathryn, I prayed for God to give me that kind of sensitivity of the Holy Spirit. In meeting after meeting with Kathryn, I watched invalids stand up and start walking. No matter what her critics might say, I witnessed absolutely phenomenal happenings. Not everybody was healed; a lot of people left the services still sick, but many received new health.

That was the public Kathryn Kuhlman. It was easy to see why people were so awestruck by her.

But there was also another side of Kathryn—the private person, the loner, whom few people knew well. During my first year of working for her, I admired the public figure while I learned to understand the private woman.

Unquestionably Kathryn liked me. Some have suggested that her feelings went deeper. If they did, I wasn't aware of them. I worked closely with her for seven years, and I knew her well. I did notice that she was telling me more intimate details of her life—nothing embarrassing or wrong. She would talk about how she felt or express concern about where her life was going. And I listened.

Kathryn liked having me around; my presence helped her feel good and probably feel younger. She was nearly forty years older than I was. Maybe she felt that while not having a mate, she at least had someone close. Nothing romantic ever went on between us, and she never initiated anything of an improper nature. Yet some people become obsessive about sex and marriage, seemingly eager to believe the worst about those who are well-known.

Whenever people interview me or talk to me for an extended period, invariably two questions emerge. The first, not always stated quite this bluntly: Did you have any romantic relationship with Kathryn Kuhlman?

"No," I always answer because that's the truth.

The second question is, What do you know about her marriage and divorce? When people first began to ask, I had been with Kathryn only a matter of weeks. The subject fascinated people, especially those who didn't know her well.

After we'd been in a city for several days, the host or someone who worked closely with us, would often ask me about Kathryn's marriage. In the beginning I'd say, "I don't know anything about it." After Kathryn began to talk to me about herself, I learned sketchy bits of information about her marriage, but I never learned much.

After that, when people questioned me, I'd tell them, "That's something you'll have to ask her about." The story of her marriage, perhaps because she didn't talk about it, intrigued people. I'm as curious as anybody else. Naturally

I heard what people thought they knew and every tale was different. One story said that she picked out a married man and deliberately tore him away from his family. Another said she met a man in one of her services and they eloped the next day. A third said he had been a married evangelist and, through their teaming up professionally, their relationship progressed and they fell in love. A few insisted that she had never married, and only her enemies had started such gossip about her.

Once we became friends, I felt free enough to ask questions about the man she had married or was supposed to have married. I'm not sure why I probed except that I wanted to know the truth, and I wanted to hear it from her.

"Kathryn, there's something I'd like to know, if you don't mind," I said one evening at her house in Fox Chapel, a subdivision close to Pittsburgh. Maggie had been with us but she had gone into another room. Kathryn and I sat in the living room and talked. "Who is this man you were married to? I've heard conflicting stories. Some say you didn't actually marry. Others said you were married for only a couple of years. Tell me, were you married or weren't you?"

"His name is Burroughs Waltrip," she said. That answer opened the door. Kathryn began to talk about him, but not then or later did she ever explain how or where they had met. I picked up the impression that he was also a preacher but she never said that. "I planned to marry him because I loved him. And I still love him."

"What happened?" I asked. "I mean, if you loved him . . . ?"

"It's my understanding that the marriage was annulled," she said vaguely.

"Why?"

"Because when I walked down the aisle I fainted at the altar," she said. "I literally passed out at the altar."

"What do you mean? You fainted?" I was a little skeptical.

"I passed out," she said. "I really did. The next thing I knew I was in a hotel room, and we were married. I told him it wasn't going to work. That the marriage wasn't what God wanted in my life. I said to him, 'This is wrong.'"

Kathryn told me that she had come to the place where she had to make a choice. By remaining with him, she would never have had a dynamic ministry. God had already started using her in the healing ministry. And, from what I've figured out from other things Kathryn said, he was one of those people completely awed by her. In Waltrip's mind he had built her up to be something more than human.

Kathryn, without embarrassment or an attempt to make him seem like a terrible person, told me they talked at length one afternoon and finally they came to an agreement.

"OK, Kathryn," he said to her, "if that's the way you want it, I'm not going to fight you. I won't force you to be my wife. I love you, and I promise to leave you alone."

Kathryn told me of a poignant scene that might have come from a movie melodrama. That evening she walked with him to the station. As he boarded a train, he blew her a kiss. Kathryn watched until the train disappeared from sight. "I've never seen him since, Dino."

With tears in her eyes, Kathryn said again that she loved him, had always loved him, and would never stop loving him. "But, Dino, I had to do it. You see, I had to put God's will first in my life."

"So you gave him up?"

"I gave myself to God," she said.

A month or so later Kathryn started talking about her marriage again. "He still loves me, Dino. I know he does." She said that through the years he had kept his promise and stayed out of her life. "But he lets me know that he's never stopped caring."

"How does he do that if he stayed away?"

"Every Christmas," she said, "I get a card from him." She explained that he never wrote his return address and the postmark was always from a different place. "But it's enough for me to know that he has never stopped loving me."

From a drawer she pulled out a simple Christmas card and handed it to me. "This is last year's," she said. "I've kept all of them."

I stared at the typical Christmas greetings. It contained no message on the inside except for two words: "Love, Walt."

"I loved him," she said again as she put the card back into the drawer, "but I love God more." The emotion in her voice and the moistness of her eyes convinced me that she meant those words.

Still curious, I asked, "Kathryn, do you have a picture of him? I'd like to see what he looks like."

She walked across the room and opened the bottom drawer of a small dresser. From where I sat I could see pictures scattered all over the inside. She sorted through them, pulled out one photograph, and brought it to me.

The moment I saw the photograph, an odd sensation overcame me.

I stared at the man in the picture, probably taken when he was in his thirties. He had black hair and was dark-complexioned like those of us of Mediterranean heritage. And though we didn't look exactly alike, our coloring and eyes were the same. I suddenly wondered if perhaps Kathryn projected some of her feelings for him on me. She had never done anything out of line, but the likeness in the photo arrested me.

I never asked about him again.

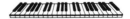

I was present when Ruth Martin introduced D.B. ("Tink") and Sue Wilkerson to Kathryn. The event ordinarily wouldn't have impressed me very much; people constantly yearned to meet Kathryn. Then while we were chatting, Tink offered Kathryn a ride on his private jet. That impressed all of us; we didn't often meet people who made such offers.

As I learned, Tink was a wealthy car dealer from Tulsa, Oklahoma. He had a number of contacts among Kathryn's friends and associates beyond Ruth and Gene Martin. The Wilkersons had also been close to Thurlow Spurr of the Spurlows—a gospel singing group. As I recall, Tink helped the Spurlows to get a national sponsorship from Chrysler for their television programs.

For years the Spurlows were a big name. They traveled throughout the United States and had several groups. Some have said that they brought the ministry of Christian entertainment to church. The women wore the long gowns and they used expert, professional lighting and sound just like the best acts in show business. They did a lot of good work in schools, in churches, and especially in reaching young people.

As I saw it, Tink liked associating with stars—the people in the spotlight. I know he and Sue strongly desired to meet Kathryn and become close to her. That's not unusual. Something about stars attracts certain types of people who just want to be close to them, to be considered friends, and they will do just about anything to get into their inner circle.

Sue was slim, attractive, with an aristocratic bearing. She wore her hair straight back and dressed fashionably. Tink was short and plump and in his mid-forties when we first met. They attended one of Kathryn's meetings, probably in Tulsa, and wanted to meet her.

From that introduction a relationship began. They contacted her regularly by phone. They worked at getting closer to Kathryn. Kathryn, aware of what they were doing, didn't brush them off. However, she told me a number of times that she never felt close to them.

Then I got to know the Wilkersons better. When Kathryn didn't need me, I set up my own concerts. Sometime during 1971 Tink stepped in and, through his assistance, I set up bookings in the Tulsa area. In fact, I played at his home church before I went anywhere else. They appeared genuinely delighted they could help. But as nice and as friendly as they were, whenever they were alone with me, they'd grill me about Kathryn. "What's it like to be close to her?" "Is she always so upbeat?" "How do you explain this ministry?"

For some reason, their unrelenting questions made me uncomfortable, even though I was used to people cornering me, wanting to know about Kathryn. After a few minutes, most of the inquirers stopped. But not the Wilkersons. As much as I tried to answer them, they never let up. Their questioning exceeded curiosity; it was more like an obsession.

Some individuals saw in Kathryn Kuhlman an image of a supernatural being, a person who was not only different in behavior, but also a little above the human level. Even some of the people who worked for Kathryn reacted with a kind of reverence.

Kathryn wasn't comfortable when anyone treated her with deference. She once said, "Dino, I don't want to be around people like that because I can't be real with them."

No one manifested the intense level of avid curiosity of Tink and Sue. After a while, when the Wilkersons came at me with their questions, I tried to be vague. "How can I answer what it's like?" Or "I suppose I should be honored. She's a great lady." One time I recall telling them, "I'm learning a lot and Kathryn has taught me many things just by letting me watch the way she works."

Regardless of my answers, they wanted more, as if they wouldn't be content until they knew every fact and intimate detail of her life.

This became clear to me when I said one time, "Kathryn has helped me a lot. I've had a lot of good experiences being with her. We've laughed, we've had fun, and we've cried together."

Tink's eyes lit up when I mentioned laughing and crying together. I sensed he savored a similar experience for himself.

No matter how much I told them, they seemed to have more questions.

As Kathryn and I became good friends, it didn't take me long to realize that the relationship between her and Ruth was going downhill. I sensed that a break between them was inevitable.

Before I came on the scene, Ruth and Kathryn had been close. They had traveled to Hong Kong together and all over Europe. Ruth had been her companion and right arm. After Kathryn hired me, just a kid from New York City who played the piano, their relationship deteriorated. For a while I wondered if I had caused the disruption between them. But I realized it would have happened eventually anyway.

I soon recognized that I was caught between two women—two powerful females who both liked me and behaved as if they had the right to control my everyday decisions and my destiny.

On the one hand, Ruth Martin considered me her discovery. After all, as Ruth mentioned frequently, she had heard me first and introduced me to Kathryn. Because of this she acted as if she had some kind of claim on me or that I owed her special loyalty.

While Ruth knew how to get things done, she was especially competent at knowing how to deal with men at places like CBS. I figured Ruth didn't like other women because she didn't work well with them.

Perhaps she didn't set it up consciously, but I noticed that Ruth Martin enjoyed having young guys around her. As one person remarked cattily, "Ruth sashays all over the place." I'm not implying immorality because I never saw her do anything out of line. I would like to say that she was just being Ruth.

Ruth's behavior toward men intrigued Kathryn, even though Kathryn never imitated her. Did Kathryn have moments when she thought, *I wish I could do that?* Possibly, but she couldn't and it wouldn't have been Kathryn if she had tried.

Although I felt no romantic attraction to Ruth, she and I got along well. She liked me, appreciated my talent, and just liked me to be around to talk to.

All the while the two women talked, planned, and worked together, I sensed a competitiveness just below the surface. Kathryn was the star and, naturally, everything on the program had to revolve around her. But since it didn't directly involve me—or so I assumed—I observed from the sidelines.

The undercurrent of rivalry festered as they both tried to take control of my life. Both liked me and liked having me around. I came off an innocent and, to them, maybe even naive—and I probably was. But I'd never been caught in a situation before where I was a young guy trying to deal with two older women.

I was uncomfortable but I treated them courteously and always as a gentleman. Increasingly I felt they were squeezing me in from both sides, at times forcing me to play both ends to keep the situation calm.

While Ruth did an admirable job for Kathryn, others began to comment and predict that their relationship couldn't possibly last much longer. Ruth turned increasingly aggressive. At times she insulted and belittled Kathryn. Finally it reached the point where Ruth said mean things to Kathryn in front of other people.

Naive as I was, I could see that Kathryn would have to replace Ruth. It never occurred to me that someone else taking over would be a big factor in my later decisions.

The Kathryn-Ruth issue came to a head in the summer of 1971. Kathryn and I had boarded a 747 at Pittsburgh to fly to Los Angeles. By then I had become a regular member of Kathryn's staff and also her friend. All that day Kathryn had seemed unusually quiet; I hadn't given it much thought.

All of a sudden, half-sobbing Kathryn said, "I can't take it anymore. This just can't go on."

Shocked at the intensity of her emotions, I had no idea what was disturbing her.

"No more of this," Kathryn continued, "She's becoming too aggressive. She's embarrassing me."

I still said nothing, but by then I had figured it out. She was referring to Ruth Martin.

"I can't take anymore from her."

That it had taken so long for her to reach that conclusion surprised me. Ruth was regularly saying harsh things to Kathryn in my presence and around others. On several occasions I wondered why Kathryn allowed her to get away with it. She would have allowed no one else to speak to her that way more than once.

"So what are you going to do?" I asked.

"I just don't know," Kathryn said. "I can't have her working for me anymore, and yet I need somebody. Somebody who's capable." She wrestled as much with finding someone else for the job as much as she did over replacing Ruth Martin.

"If you feel you have to replace Ruth . . ."

"Dino, I don't have a choice anymore," she said flatly.

"I just had an idea," I said, "and it might work."

"Oh? What's that?"

"It occurred to me that you might be interested in hiring Paul Bartholomew, my brother-in-law. He's an administrator for several schools in upstate New York. Paul could handle Ruth's work." I didn't need to say much more about him because Kathryn knew a great deal about all my family members.

"Ohhh, that would be wonderful!"

"If you're determined Ruth has to go . . ." I left the sentence unfinished. While interested in helping my family, I honestly didn't want it to come about by shoving out someone else.

"She's finished," Kathryn said with finality. "I won't tolerate her ever again. Not ever! Now, tell me more about Paul."

I told her about Paul's background and education. Then she wanted to know the names of his and Chris's six children and all the family details. But by then, I knew this line of questioning was characteristic of Kathryn. As we talked, the situation seemed right. She had been impressed with my family loyalty from the beginning. Also, Paul wanted to work in some form of ministry.

"OK, call him. Today," she said in her rapid decision-making tone. She had never met Paul and didn't know anything other than what I had told her. "Let's fly him out here.

I want him to take over. Immediately." The flight to L.A. was over; we were home.

I had no way of knowing that while we had solved one problem, we were creating new ones.

Chapter 11

CONTROLLING INTERESTS

Within an hour of our arrival in Los Angeles, I phoned New York to tell Paul that Kathryn wanted to hire him. He agreed to consider it, and Kathryn had him on a plane the next morning. Everything happened quickly because Kathryn was desperate and unhappy.

As soon as Paul arrived in Los Angeles, I took him out to see Kathryn. I introduced them, they said a few words and then she said crisply, "Paul, you're in. Ruth is out."

The situation had gotten so tense between the two women that Kathryn didn't want to talk to Ruth. "You're in charge now," Kathryn told Paul. "You move her out of there. Today."

Located in a chic area called Fashion Island in Newport Beach, the sign said it was the Ruth Martin Agency but Kathryn paid the bills. So, along with the position, Paul inherited the suite of offices, which Kathryn had had beautifully decorated. The outside walls were glass all around and provided an excellent view of Newport Beach and the ocean.

Hired as Kathryn's administrator, Paul took over and moved Ruth Martin. Ruth left graciously without giving Paul any trouble. Movers came in and pulled out everything that belonged to the Martin Agency. Before nightfall a new sign read "Bartholomew Agency."

Because Paul was family and I grew up believing we do what we can to take care of family, it seemed perfectly natural for me to suggest him. Family is important. I love my relatives and I would die for them. Among traditional Greeks, blood is thick. Yet if I had known Kathryn was going to move so quickly and with such finality, I probably wouldn't have recommended Paul. The day Paul came in, Kathryn instructed him to notify all the stations handling her programs that they would no longer deal with the Ruth Martin Agency. I felt bad for Ruth because Kathryn had been one of her big accounts, possibly her largest.

This new job was also quite a move for Paul and Chris, his wife. At the time, Paul was in his early thirties. They sold their home in Cambridge, New York, uprooted their family, and moved to California immediately. Paul suddenly had his own agency, and although he worked for Kathryn on a commission, he made good money. Paul and Chris bought a fine house in a good community. But their kids hated California and had a hard time adjusting. It was a traumatic experience for them to be pulled away so quickly and without any preparation.

Within a week after Paul began working for Kathryn, conflict arose. While Paul did his work well, Kathryn didn't like him. I've never been sure why the two didn't get on well. As soon as Paul walked into the room, Kathryn spoke to him with an edge in her voice.

One day Kathryn called me aside. "I don't like Paul coming to see me any more," she said.

"He could phone I suppose . . ."

"He doesn't need to phone me either."

"But how can he do his job?" I asked. "He has to be in close contact with you."

"Paul can tell you everything I need to know," she said. The manner in which she spoke told me that she was adamant.

"All right," I said, understanding what she wanted. From then on I became the buffer. Since Paul was family, I played the go-between, without arguing with Kathryn over the craziness of the situation. The way Kathryn originally set up things, I worked under Paul, yet she started sending all her directives through me. To his credit, Paul didn't lash out in anger after I told him what Kathryn had decided. Naturally, Paul resented the treatment, but he took it.

Unfortunately, that didn't end the trouble. Despite my trying to be the peacemaker, Kathryn didn't like many of the decisions Paul made. More than once she would say, "That is unacceptable. Tell him."

As the alienation continued to grow, Kathryn leaned more on me. I was young, unattached, flattered by the attention, and I enjoyed having someone rely on my judgment. Yet I felt caught between Kathryn, my friend and employer, and Paul, my brother-in-law. Despite her feelings about Paul, Kathryn made it clear that she didn't plan to fire him. Paul didn't speak of quitting. I couldn't see any resolution for the problem.

At that time it never occurred to me that Kathryn might have hired Paul for the unconscious motive to bind me closer to her. But it occurred to Paul. Within two weeks after Paul moved to California, he was aware of what was going on. He told Chris but neither of them said anything to me. Either I was slow to catch on or chose to ignore what was happening. I still hadn't realized it, but Kathryn was slowly trying to control my life.

In retrospect, I can plainly see the events bound me, step-by-step, to Kathryn. I had replaced Ruth as her confidant. Then my brother-in-law became her administrator

Dino's ministry and message display both grandeur and peace.

On the Pianorama set at TBN.

Dino and the Pianorama players.

"Peace in the Midst of the Storm" video (above).

Cheryl, Dino, and Thurlow Spurr plan the video for "Peace" (below).

Dino on the set at the TBN taping of "The Dino Show."

YaYa and Dino at the piano in the Sixty-Third Street apartment.

Dino and his family: sister Christine, father John, mother Helen, and Dino (left to right).

Sister Christine, YaYa, Aunt Angie, Helen, and Dino (above).

The apartment at Sixty-Third Street and Amsterdam Avenue. The Lincoln Center has replaced the old Kartsonakis' family dwelling.

YaYa and Dino at the luncheonette (below).

The Lincoln Luncheonette, Dino's father's business (above).

YaYa wears black at her son's gravesight.

After YaYa became a Christian, she no longer wore black.

When Dino was fifteen, he played for a teen gospel quartet called the Christian Keynotes and experienced some of his first tours.

Sister Marie Brown, pastor of Glad Tidings Tabernacle.

Aunt Evangeline (Angie) and Uncle Joe DeJulio. Kathryn supported their mission work in Crete.

Kathryn's ministry took her to the Vatican to meet the Pope.

Kathryn Kuhlman—employer, confidante, friend, and inspiration.

Kathryn, Dino, and YaYa (left to right). Kathryn especially loved YaYa.

Helen and John Kartsonakis (Mom and Dad); Maggie Hartner, Kathryn Kuhlman, and YaYa (left to right).

Tink and Sue Wilkerson at Ruth Martin's house.

Ruth Martin, a bottom-line woman, who opened the door to Dino's years with Kathryn.

Sue Wilkerson and Ruth Martin.

In the winter of 1989, Dino traveled to China.

Dino, missionary Nora Lam, and Cheryl (left to right) at the Great Wall (above). And Dino at housechurch with Pastor Ling, Nora, and Cheryl (left).

Dino goes beyond the glitz to build a hospital in Haiti.

*Dino and the girls enjoy
Thanksgiving at the
Matterhorn.*

*The Kartsonakis girls,
Cheri and Christina.*

and, consequently, dependent upon her for his income. Shortly afterward, Kathryn insisted I play in practically all of her meetings. I still held my own concerts but I was finding fewer open dates for them.

Then Kathryn began to invite me, along with Maggie, when she vacationed. When she extended the invitation she emphasized my need for rest. Once when she was going to South America for a week, she said "Dino, you work too hard. Maggie and I are going to take a few days to relax. I think you ought to come too. You don't have to work all the time."

When she scheduled a business meeting in another part of the country, she'd ask me to go along, "because you have such good common sense, Dino. And with your commitment to God, I trust your judgment."

Increasingly, Kathryn identified herself with my family. Although Mom and Kathryn were never intimate, the relationship between YaYa and Kathryn was special from the moment they met. Kathryn frequently telephoned her. Whenever she visited New York, she made it a point to contact YaYa.

My grandmother looked like an old-time Pentecostal with her hair tied back in a bun, no makeup, and simply-styled, yet colorful, clothes.

YaYa loved Kathryn because she recognized how she helped me; YaYa also loved her because of her ministry. As a matter of fact, I've often thought of my grandmother as a Kathryn Kuhlman type through whom God performed miracles. Like Kathryn, she knew God and God spoke to her. Kathryn sensed that same type of spirit in YaYa.

This much I do know: Kathryn looked up to YaYa as a spiritual giant. Kathryn frequently telephoned YaYa and asked, "Will you pray for me?"

I recall half a dozen times when Kathryn said, "Whenever I need prayer, YaYa is the one I go to. She's such a woman of God."

Interestingly enough, the two women couldn't communicate well with each other because YaYa spoke little English. When I mentioned that to Kathryn she said, "Dino, the presence of God surrounds your grandmother. That's the only language I need."

Another time Kathryn said, "Your grandmother is a real prayer warrior. When she prays, things happen."

After we talked a little about some of the remarkable things that came about after YaYa prayed, Kathryn said, "As long as YaYa's alive, you've got nothing to worry about."

After my parents moved to California, I kept trying to get YaYa to fly out to the West Coast for a visit. She always refused.

I persisted. She had never flown before, so I told her, "YaYa, you've got to learn to go places." Finally, one day she said, "The only way I'll fly is if Kathryn will sit next to me."

I thought that was funny. Still laughing about it, I told Kathryn what my grandmother had said. Kathryn beamed.

A few days later, without saying a word to anyone, Kathryn flew to New York and returned the next afternoon—with my grandmother!

What were Kathryn's motives in all the things she did for me and my family? I won't try to explain them. Some of them were obviously inspired by genuine affection for me and my family. But as time progressed, I began to suspect that other motives were at work, motives that Kathryn herself probably didn't realize.

Then another binding cord took hold.

One day Kathryn and I were talking about the mission field, and I mentioned my Aunt Angie. At Eastern Bible Institute she met and later married an Italian named Joe De Julio. Joe learned Greek and they went as missionaries to Greece as often as possible and for as long as possible. They yearned to go full-time, but since they didn't have financial support, they stayed until their funds ran out and then returned to America. They worked until they again collected enough funds to go back.

I admired their commitment. "I'd like to be able to help them," I was saying, trying to figure how much I could afford to send them each month.

"I can help," Kathryn said. "You know I believe in missions." And, of course, she did and gave generously.

At first I was embarrassed because I didn't want Kathryn to think I had brought up the topic so that she would volunteer her money. When I mentioned that, she pushed it aside and assured me that she hadn't even considered such a thing.

"Oh, sure, we'll support them," Kathryn said rather calmly. "Whatver they need each month, I'll send it—100 percent."

"Kathryn, that could be quite a chunk of money."

"It's for God's kingdom, isn't it? And for really committed people?"

"You won't find anybody more committed."

"Then it's settled. We'll support them."

I could hardly believe she would jump like that so I asked, "Are you sure you want to do this? You don't even know them."

"I'm sure," she said. "You find out how much they need to live in Greece and then let me know."

The news made Aunt Angie and Uncle Joe ecstatic. As soon as they began to receive funds from Kathryn, they flew back to the island of Crete, rented an apartment, and exerted a remarkable influence among the people. True to her word, Kathryn provided their total income. Since my aunt and uncle worked with the Assemblies of God, every month Kathryn sent a check for their support to the denominational headquarters.

Even my Uncle Angelo Frudakis got involved with Kathryn. Like the other things that happened, their meeting wasn't anything I calculated. Instead, the event came about when I mentioned to Kathryn that I had never seen a real portrait of her.

"No paintings of me," she replied.

"Then you ought to have someone sculpt you."

"On, no," she laughed. "I don't want any monuments left of me after I die."

Suddenly, I had another idea. "How about a coin or something to give to your supporters? Something that's personal and memorable? You know, your picture on a key chain or a money clip—something your supporters could look at and hold. It would remind them to pray for you."

"Now that might work," she said.

Kathryn was always looking for new ideas. Also, she had mentioned that she wanted something she could offer her faithful radio audience as a gift. As she considered my suggestion, the idea took on more appeal for her.

Kathryn finally settled on having a special coin made, the size of a half dollar, with her portrait on it.

"Say, you might ask my Uncle Angelo to do that."

"The one who's a sculptor?"

"That's the one." Uncle Angelo Frudakis is a renowned sculptor in Philadelphia. Although Kathryn had never met him, like all of my relatives, I'd mentioned Uncle Angelo often.

The next day Kathryn commissioned Uncle Angelo to do her portrait—on a coin. This task posed nothing new for Uncle Angelo who had previously done a series on the life of Christ for The Franklin Mint.

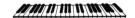

I was in my late twenties when I went to work for Kathryn Kuhlman. As much as I enjoyed working with her, I had never considered being employed by her for the rest of my life. Kathryn had always known that eventually I planned to be on my own as an independent artist. During my seven years with Kathryn I did concerts on my own, with her knowledge. Occasionally, she introduced me to contacts or actually suggested that a church ask me to come. I made it clear that, as one of the first steps toward my independence, I was building up my list of contacts.

I also figured I would be getting married one day and raising a family. Staying forever single had no appeal to me. One time when I mentioned this, Kathryn cautioned me, "Just be sure, Dino. Just be sure God leads you to the right person." At the time I simply interpreted that statement as advice from a friend who had been through her own marital tragedy and wanted to spare me.

By the time I had become financially secure enough to think about marriage, I realized that a subtle change had taken place in our relationship. Although I had seen Kathryn's possessiveness in her dealings with others, more than four years passed before I became aware of what she was doing to my life.

I can trace my shift of awareness to the time I started dating Christian women, after I got settled into the ministry. None of my dates developed into significant relationships, but I enjoyed meeting women and hoped that, along the way, I would discover the right woman for me.

I mentioned my first few dates to Kathryn. Each time she warned me against ruining my life by marrying the wrong person. I listened, still assuming she was reacting from her own sad love life. It didn't occur to me how seriously she was involving herself in my personal affairs. After a few months of hearing the same sermon, I stopped telling Kathryn about my dates. It didn't matter, as I soon learned, because she had spies who kept her informed.

People actually reported to her when they saw me with a woman. Even though I had stopped talking about my dates, I didn't do anything secretive. The networking of her spy system should have been obvious, but such an idea didn't enter my head.

Dating back as early as the winter of 1970, when Kathryn learned I had been out with a woman—and she always knew by the next day—she called me aside to speak about confidential matters. During the conversation she interjected something like, "Dino, you have a special gift from God. Be careful you don't allow someone—some woman—to take you away from God's best." Usually the remarks were that simple and subtle. Only occasionally did she go as far as to say, "That young lady that I've heard you're dating—she just isn't right for you."

Besides the eager reporters, Kathryn quizzed my friends until she learned everything about the current woman in my life and how to get in touch with her. Then Kathryn "helped" me—not that she ever asked me—by getting rid of another "wrong woman" in my life. Usually she accomplished this with nothing more than a telephone call.

Because this went on behind my back, I dated a number of women who became cool and distant after only a few days. Occasionally, one of my dates and I seemed to hit it off well, but, after a few dates, she didn't want to see me again. I wondered why and felt confused about the abrupt change of attitude. Only later, when I began to date Casia did I discover what had been happening.

One day Kathryn brought a beautiful young woman named Casia to the studio. Casia was a high-fashion model whose picture had appeared on the cover of *Vogue* and other top magazines. She had impressed Kathryn and the two seemed to get along well.

The first time Casia appeared on the television program, Kathryn introduced her as "this lovely Christian who is a top model for the best fashion magazines." As I listened, I kept thinking how beautiful she was. She sang and played a guitar. Because the audience responded favorably, Kathryn asked Casia to appear on additional shows.

As I saw her around more, I started talking with Casia. I liked her wholesomeness immediately. She was not only beautiful but a warm person. When I asked her out for dinner, she accepted. We had a lovely evening because Casia was easy to open up to and the conversation flowed. Sitting across the table from her, I thought, *This is the kind of person I could easily fall in love with.*

But we didn't get that far.

After the third date, Ruth phoned me. Even though she wasn't working for Kathryn, she still seemed to know about my romantic life. "Dino," she said, "I want to tell you something. I hope you don't mind, but it's something for your own good."

"Oh? What is it?"

"You've been going out with Casia, haven't you?"

"I sure have. She's one of the nicest women I've ever known," I said enthusiastically, assuming she was pleased about our getting together. "We've had several delightful dates, just talking and enjoying being with each other. She's a warm, caring person and . . ."

"No! That's wrong" she interrupted. "You shouldn't be dating her."

"Why not?"

"Kathryn isn't going to like it. That's why. You'd better stop seeing Casia."

"I can't believe you're telling me this." It was the first time I remember feeling angry toward Ruth. "What business do you have trying to run my life? Telling me I shouldn't date someone?"

"I'm not interfering or trying to run your life, Dino. I'm just saying that Kathryn won't like it!" Her words sounded like a threat.

"What's the big deal?" I asked. "Casia and I just like each other. We're not in love. Why would Kathryn be upset?"

"She just would. She'd think you were ruining your career and turning your back on your talent."

"Casia is a Christian. She wants to serve the Lord . . ."

"Kathryn likes Casia. She's been on the show, hasn't she? It's just that Kathryn wants God's will for your life. And believe me, Casia is not the woman God wants you to marry."

"Who are you to tell me who is and who isn't God's will for me?" My body tingled with anger for a few minutes. What right did she have to do that? She wasn't my mother, nor was my date life any of her business. I fumed silently.

Later I cooled off and thought more about it. While I liked Casia, if Kathryn thought she wasn't the right person for me, I wondered if I should listen to her. Perhaps God had spoken to Kathryn. I had already seen her supernatural gifts at work. I didn't have to wonder for long what to do.

I asked Casia for another date, but she refused: "Let's just not see each other again."

"Look," I said, genuinely surprised at her response, "the other night we had a good time. Is there anything I've done to offend you?"

"It's nothing you've done, Dino."

"Then why don't you want to go out with me again?"

"Maybe you'd better ask Ruth Martin . . . or Kathryn."

"What do they have to do with whether you go out with me?"

"Ruth Martin called me yesterday. That's what it has to do with you."

"What are you talking about?" I couldn't believe Ruth would actually interfere in my private life. She wasn't even working for Kathryn, and we had virtually no contact.

"She doesn't want me to go out with you again. She said quite clearly, 'I want you to stay away from Dino. Your relationship isn't going anyplace. You'd better know it right now before you get too involved and end up getting hurt.'"

I don't remember what or how I answered, but I thanked her for telling me. As I listened, I felt the anger rising. Ruth wouldn't have done that on her own. Kathryn would have had to be behind it. After hanging up, I thought of other women who had turned me down after two or three dates. *Is that what's been going on?* I asked myself.

Kathryn had cut off Ruth Martin without any warning. Evidently Ruth was hanging on to Kathryn by phoning her and feeding her information about anyone I was dating. As far as I know, I was their only topic of conversation. Since I hadn't developed any strong feelings toward Casia, I decided to stop dating her. Yet I knew that despite what Ruth said or what Kathryn might have thought, had I become seriously involved with Casia, I would have pursued the relationship anyway.

Kathryn never again used Casia on her shows. And she never again mentioned Casia's name. It was as if Casia never existed.

That was the eye-opener for me. From then on, I clearly saw how the system was working. As soon as I became interested in a woman, Ruth would phone me and start talking about her. Time after time, I'd wonder how Ruth knew who she was. When I asked, she'd say either "I have my sources" or "You have friends who care deeply about you. They don't want you to mess up your life. They tell me when they see you starting to do that."

On other occasions, Kathryn would casually mention the importance of staying true to our ministry, to listen carefully to God speaking, and to be faithful to the gifts God had given to us.

If I continued to date the same person, Ruth and Kathryn varied their approach—and, again, it took a while for me to catch on. Both of them started calling me on the phone about insignificant matters, sometimes two or three times each day. Ruth, who was quite direct, often asked, "Hey, Dino, what are you doing now?"

Not the question but the way she asked made me feel as if her purpose in phoning had been to check up on me and to make sure I wasn't with a girl.

The calls increased. On my day off, it wasn't unusual to hear from Kathryn six or seven times over a period of eight hours. "We need you to check out the music today," Kathryn would typically say. While her calls always referred to a current situation, I knew we didn't need to have it done then.

Because I respected Kathryn and the gifts God had given her, I refused for a long time to see the obvious. I had come from a church background where we were constantly admonished, "Do not touch My anointed ones, And do My prophets no harm." To think or feel critical of Kathryn would have been, for me, hurting the anointed of the Lord.

I had also been raised to respect women and to treat them properly, so I didn't want to accuse Kathryn unjustly or angrily. The women I had known as I grew up were like my mother and YaYa—strong women who had only my good at heart. Kathryn was a new type of powerful female.

I kept asking myself, *How could Ruth and Kathryn interfere with my life like that? Who are they to decide who I can't date?*

The coils of Kathryn's possessiveness were wrapping around me and starting to squeeze tightly. Over the seven-year period we worked together, Kathryn had become increasingly possessive of every part of my life. I hadn't allowed her to control me yet, however; and I wasn't going to give in now.

I'm going to have to leave, I finally admitted to myself. *I can't let this keep going.* I had no desire to hurt Kathryn, but despite my feelings, I knew she would see my leaving as a rejection of her. I knew she would believe I was turning my back on her ministry and running away from my own.

It would not be easy for either of us. It was just a matter of time.

Chapter 12

DEMANDS AND COSTS

"Oh-h, you'll be here with Maggie and me for Thanksgiving, won't you?" Kathryn asked. Without fail, every Christmas, Thanksgiving, and other holiday, Kathryn insisted that I be around to celebrate the holiday with her.

"It won't be a real holiday without you," she said when she saw my hesitation.

The first year she asked me to stay around for holiday periods, I was genuinely flattered that she liked me and my work that much. In the following years, I began to feel sorry for her. Most people respected Kathryn, even envied her, but she had almost no friends.

After my folks moved to California, I found myself hurrying through activities with my family so I could go to Kathryn's house.

Kathryn continued inviting me to go places with her. At one point, she started calling when she decided to do a simple thing like drive across town for a business meeting, or she would insist on my presence when she made a flight to the East Coast. Always something.

Kathryn expected me to be on call, to be ready to go or do whatever she wanted. For a long time I didn't mind because I felt it was my job, my part of the ministry. *If it makes her comfortable and happy,* I said to myself, *it's better for her ministry, and it's a way I can serve the Lord.*

After I had been with Kathryn about five years, I began feeling trapped. I genuinely liked Kathryn and had enjoyed working with her. But I began to resent her control of my schedule, and I dreaded hearing the telephone ring.

Occasionally, in our conversations, Kathryn mentioned being betrayed. I remember one particular conversation that took place in 1974. "That's why I must be careful about my friends," she said. "I've had to learn through sad experiences. Many seemed so sincere, but in time I had to admit that they weren't willing to pay the price for the call of God."

I knew exactly what she was saying to me, even though indirectly. Subtly she was telling me that if I quit, I would be betraying her because I wasn't willing to give up everything to serve Jesus Christ.

"Sometimes God leads people in different directions," I responded and then mentioned that Paul and Barnabas in the Bible split up after their first missionary journey.

"Yes, but they quarreled. One of them must have been missing God's will," she was quick to point out.

I didn't answer.

Being as perceptive as Kathryn was, she must have sensed what was going on inside of me. Perhaps she knew even before I did.

Churches like Glad Tidings Tabernacle drill into their members that they are to give their lives in service to Jesus Christ. The worst sin for anyone was to turn his back on serving God. At times, a few preachers have seemed to use that commitment message as emotional or psychological blackmail to keep people in line. Because of those values taught me in my childhood, I struggled with my decision to leave Kathryn.

If I leave, will I be denying God's call? I wondered. Will I destroy God's plan for my life? *God has opened the door for me to work with Kathryn. If I pull away, will I harm her ministry? Am I allowing my heart to harden so that I don't want to hear God?*

As long as I struggled with these issues, I was caught.

About that time I took a closer look at Kathryn's lifestyle. She had collected invaluable antiques and possessed beautiful art pieces and quality jewelry. That was fine for her and didn't bother me. As a matter of fact, I admired her taste. As she grew older, I realized that Kathryn attached herself to her antiques and valuables. Maybe they compensated for her not having a normal life that included a family and close friends. I decided that if this brought her pleasure, why not? She worked hard and deserved some outlet.

Yet even that part of her life started to cause me problems.

On several occasions when I visited her house, Kathryn would hold up a vase or a figurine. "If anything happens to me," she would say, "Dino, I want you to have this."

The first time this happened, I was embarrassed and confused. "Nothing's going to happen to you for a long, long time," I said.

"But if it does," she answered, "I want to make sure you get this."

"Kathryn, I don't want any of your things."

"But, Dino, you are my friend. You've been a loyal and faithful friend. Don't you see that I want to do this? By giving it to you, I can show you how much I appreciate you and value your ministry."

When she made a point of insisting, I did the polite thing: I thanked her. But I never had any real interest in her valuable collections.

This scene took place four or five times, and on each occasion she offered me something different. When Kathryn talked that way, she became quite emotional, and I decided that she might already be thinking of her death. Only much later was I able to look back and accept the fact that Kathryn was holding up valuable objects as attempts to bind me. They were a veiled way of saying, "Dino, if you stay with my ministry, I'll reward you well. I'll leave all these lovely things for you."

Because she became more attached to them, she mistakenly assumed that I felt the same way. At one point I said to Paul Bartholomew, "I don't want to be around when Kathryn's possessions are divided. They're valuable, I guess, and expensive, but I don't want any of them."

"It's easy to put your energy into things," Paul said, "when you don't have family."

Paul's an observer of people. I don't recall his ever saying much about Kathryn until that day.

"Collecting art treasures means a lot to her," he said. Then he said he had been aware of this tendency in Kathryn for a long time. "And it is sad, isn't it?"

That conversation opened the door for me to tell Paul how I had been feeling about her interference in my love life and her constant checking up on me. "I want to do what's right," I said. "I just want to be sure I know God's will before I act."

Paul wisely didn't tell me what to do, but he did ask, "What are you going to do?"

"Kathryn wants me to do well," I said, "but she can't understand how I can be loyal to her and still have my own desires and ambitions."

"You think you ought to stay?" Paul asked.

I shook my head and talked about getting married and having children. "I want something more than what I have now. By staying with her, I'm being deprived of a normal life."

Paul nodded in understanding. "No woman will ever be good enough for you in Kathryn's eyes."

"I'm afraid you're right," I said. "And I don't want to wake up at age forty-five and ask, 'Is this all there is for me in life?' I want a wife, a family of my own."

"Then you've got a tough decision to make," Paul said.

"And one I'm going to make soon," I answered. "I'll keep you posted." Without my saying so, we both knew that if I left, Kathryn would fire him.

I knew that something would have to happen in the near future. Either Kathryn would let up or I'd leave. But I hoped that conditions would improve.

In 1971 I went to Bethel Temple in Sacramento to give a concert. There, I ran into the sound engineer for Bethel Temple, Dee Keener. Originally from Arkansas, Dee and his wife, Nita, had never lost that warmth and friendliness often associated with people from the South. Dee talked about his daughter, Debby, who he said was pretty and not involved with anyone.

I had heard similar comments about women for quite a while and from a lot of different people. As I neared thirty and was still unattached, people constantly wanted to set me up with a date. And most of them knew just the perfect wife for me. Not that I didn't want a wife—I just wanted to do my own choosing.

Yet, in practically every church where I got to know the people, somebody had a sister, daughter, or a friend. Occasionally, I received dinner invitations and ended up sitting across from a person that my host or hostess said, "You two are going to hit it off." My dinner companions were always nice, but nothing ever developed as a result.

When Dee talked about his daughter, I didn't show much interest. I had heard it all before.

Then Dee explained that Debby had grown up in the church, and after high school she enrolled at ORU (Oral Roberts University) and sang for a short time with the group at ORU called the World Action Singers. "But I guess something was eating away at Debby," her father said. "She wanted to become a star."

She left Tulsa and moved to Hollywood. A modeling agency signed her up and she did TV commercials.

"Yes, and we lost her," Nita Keener said. "When she went to Hollywood, she moved around with the wrong crowd."

As I listened to them talk about their daughter, I thought, *This daughter must have been pretty sharp—pretty enough to do commercials and sharp enough to make it with all the competition out there. It's sad she's not using her talents for the Lord.*

Minutes before the concert that evening, Dee and I were rehearsing the sound check for the last time. From the corner of my eye, I spotted a woman coming down the aisle. With a second glance, I took in how pretty she was—tall, attractive, and she was smiling. She had long, light brown hair and brown eyes. That was Debby. As she introduced herself to me, the exuberance of her personality immediately registered. She had the kind of personality that commanded attention.

After just a few minutes of speaking with her, I was even more impressed. She said she had come home for the weekend, had heard of me, and wanted to hear me play.

She soon left but in that brief exchange it was obvious that her parents hadn't exaggerated. Debby was unique.

After the concert, the Keeners, Debby, and I spent a little time together. Her openness about herself amazed me as she talked about how she strayed from God and tried to pursue a career, but she told me that most of all she wanted to get on track with God again.

I had to return to Los Angeles and, since she had seemed so involved in her career, I didn't consider her for a date once I returned to Los Angeles.

Then three years later, 1974, Debby Keener came into my life for the second time.

"Hi, Dino," she said. "How are you doing?"

I had been concentrating on last-minute details for a concert and hadn't heard her come in. I whirled around and saw Debby, as pretty as ever.

"You probably don't remember me," she said, "But I'm . . ."

"Debby," I finished for her and then realized I was staring.

That night I took her out to dinner after the concert. We talked for hours. At one point she started telling me about a brother who had been killed in a rafting accident. As she spoke, her eyes filled with tears, and I realized that his death had touched her deeply. We talked a long time about the other hurts in her life.

She was open about who she was and the kind of life she had led. She told me that she had dated Keith Hefner (brother of the famous Hugh Hefner of *Playboy*).

Debby had also dated Ed Ames, the singer and the man who played the Indian sidekick on the old "Davy Crockett" TV show. At that time she was singing backup to Dick Haymes in Las Vegas. By the time we said goodnight I knew a great deal about Debby. Her openness absolutely amazed me. Although we were nearly the same age, she had lived a lot more than I had. Beginning that night and during the months we dated, Debby continued to tell me about her past and her years away from God.

"But now I want to serve God," she said, and I loved hearing those words.

I thought about her often. Debby Keener is one of those fortunate individuals who seemed to meet people effortlessly—so different from me. She also has the ability to put them at ease. As I would see in the days ahead, Debby could walk into a room of strangers and before the evening concluded, she would know most of them. People responded to the same qualities of warmth and friendliness that I liked about her.

Debby has a compulsion to be the life of the party. I envied that because, frankly, at that time in my life I wanted to party, to have fun, to enjoy being around people my own age. I was tired of being involved in little else aside from my uptight work schedule. Debby entered my life just when I needed someone to show me the lighter side of life.

Debby was still doing TV commercials although an ad for Tupperware was the only one I ever saw. She hadn't made the big time, but she had lined up enough jobs here and there in advertising to pay her bills.

After the Sacramento concert I returned to Los Angeles and Debby did too. She let me know that she liked me, which gave me the courage to ask, "How about dinner next week?"

"I'd love it."

"I'll call you as soon as I get back and look at my schedule," I said.

From that point on, we began to date regularly, seeing each other as often as our schedules allowed. To my surprise I found I was falling in love.

What attracted me to Debby Keener? How can I say for sure? I can figure out a few things. First, Debby possessed a powerful personality, like the women who had already played significant roles in my life.

Second, and probably more important, I was getting anxious to move away from Kathryn's control. Being a man of normal desires, I wanted a wife. I wanted to settle down and live my life my way and not as an extension of Kathryn Kuhlman.

Third, maybe a little missionary zeal went into our relationship. I'd never strayed from God, but I discovered I could have a chance to help someone who had. That appealed to my desire to serve God and to help others—as I'd been taught to do all my life. Please understand, I wasn't conscious of such a motive, and I can admit it only in retrospect. At the time I was conscious of only one thing—Debby Keener was the best thing that had happened to me since I had started to work for Kathryn in 1969.

Debby was the first girl I felt free to talk with, to really open myself up to, and we enjoyed being together. She encouraged me to talk and to be myself. I admired her playfulness which was such a contrast to everything else around me.

In the meantime Debby was slowly changing her lifestyle, trying to live like a Christian. She had been going to church and was starting to get involved in that—although her circle of friends were still predominantly show-business types.

I loved Debby and wanted to marry her. I felt that she loved me. I knew we would have a wonderful life together so I decided to do something about our relationship. I drove to Las Vegas to see her in the Dick Haymes show. Afterward we had dinner together.

I reached across the table, took her hand in mine, and looked deep into her eyes. "I love you," I said. "I love you and I want to marry you."

"I love you, too, Dino," she whispered, her eyes shining. Then she simply answered, "Yes, I'll marry you."

With my heart pounding I slipped the ring on her finger. Later when we told her parents, they were ecstatic.

"Now Debby is really going to shape up," her dad said. "And God's going to use her."

Chapter 13

A BIG DECISION

Debby was now going to church faithfully, and we openly shared about God in our lives. Everything seemed wonderful; I couldn't see how it would ever change.

My continuing to date Debby was hard on Kathryn, however. She marshaled every weapon against our relationship, which included her repeating every story she had ever heard about Debby. "You're making a big mistake," she would say. "She isn't for you."

"I've heard a rumor," Kathryn said one morning, "that Debby used to be a Playboy bunny and lived in the Playboy mansion."

"I've heard that rumor too," I said. "And I don't believe it."

"Why not?"

"Because I asked Debby and she said it wasn't true."

"And you believed her?"

"I still believe her," I said. "Listen, Debby has talked so openly to me about her past, why would she lie about involvement with the Playboy people?"

"Oh, Dino, Dino . . ."

"Besides, Kathryn, I don't care about her past. I love her for who she is now."

"People don't change!" Kathryn said angrily. "If she was that way ten years ago, she's that way today."

"We're all human," I said. "We all have weaknesses. But God forgives. God enables us to change."

"Not our basic nature," she insisted. "That stays the same."

I felt pushed to defend myself and the relationship, yet it didn't do any good. I could finally see that no woman would ever meet Kathryn's approval. I resented her meddling, and I wonder now if her push to destroy my relationship with Debby didn't actually push me closer to Debby.

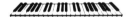

Twice I tactfully tried to explain to Kathryn how I felt, but it didn't do any good. She still saw my romantic life as part of her ministry. "I'm concerned for you. I want only God's best in your life, Dino. I wish you could understand that, when I know you're making a mistake, I have to tell you."

"Kathryn, thank you," I said, "but I don't want to be told."

During this period, my parents were particularly supportive. I was thankful that rather than offer advice, they stood by me.

"I'll have to live with God over my own choices," I told Dad and Mom. "I love Debby and I think we have a future together."

"Do what you feel God wants you to do," Dad said. "No matter what you do or what happens, we'll always be with you."

Early spring, 1975, everything was coming to a head. Debby and I had dinner one night at Five Crowns, a lovely place at Newport Beach. Afterward, Debby had to drive to Sacramento to see her folks.

Three hours after Debby and I had parted, her mother phoned me.

"Dino, Debby's in the UCLA hospital in Los Angeles. She's been in an accident on the highway." Although Nita was worried about her daughter, she assured me it wasn't life threatening.

Ruth Martin found out about the accident, and she phoned Kathryn who was in Pittsburgh.

"How much do you know about Debby Keener?" were Kathryn's first words to me on the phone. "How much do you *really* know about her?"

"Enough," I said. "She's been open about her past and she wants to serve the Lord. That's all I care about."

"Open with you?" I could hear a mixture of anger and pain in her voice as she said this. "Do you know who is paying her medical expenses?"

"I hadn't thought about it," I said. "I suppose she has insurance . . ."

"No! Not insurance." Kathryn lowered her voice and said, "Hugh Hefner is paying all the expenses. For someone who was never involved in the Playboy mansion, that sounds strange to me. And Mr. Hefner is paying for everying. What do you suppose it's costing him? Debby isn't in just any room, Dino, she . . ."

"I know. She has a suite," I said.

"Not just any suite. She's on the top floor of the UCLA Hospital!"

I could hardly believe what I was hearing. I resented Kathryn for finding out about Debby's suite and calling to report to me. But I forced myself to stay calm and said, "Debby and I aren't married, you know. It's not any of my business."

"It isn't? You've been dating her steadily now. She's been telling you about her walk with Jesus Christ. Does this sound like a woman who's following the Lord?"

Questions and doubts started to fill my mind and when I realized what Kathryn was doing, I said, "OK, so he's paying. Debby probably doesn't have insurance . . ."

"But Hugh Hefner?"

"That's still *her* business," I said, gripping the phone.

"You're going to have a lot of problems," she yelled into the phone.

"Then I'll have problems. *My* problems."

I had wanted Kathryn to come around so that I could marry Debby and continue to play for Kathryn. I finally realized that was not going to happen. I prepared to quit.

When I first hinted that I was leaving, Kathryn became upset. "You think it's easy out there?" she asked. "You think people will come to hear just anybody? Just let me see you go out there and draw five thousand people."

Not only was she trying to control my personal life, I realized, she was trying to control my destiny. It seemed Kathryn was saying, "If you leave *me,* you're not going to be able to draw a lot of people by yourself. You'll have crowds at your concerts, but it's only because of your connection to Kathryn Kuhlman. If you're smart, you'll stick with me."

Working for Kathryn had been an extraordinary opportunity for me to develop my ministry and had given me a platform so that people recognized me. I'll always be thankful for the chance she gave me. But I realized there was more for me in life than playing for Kathryn.

In late February 1975, I phoned Paul. "Get ready," I said, "It's not going to be long." He knew what I meant.

I wanted to give Paul some warning because I felt responsible for him. I had brought him into Kathryn's ministry and owed him the chance to start making career provisions for himself and his family.

"I can't allow Kathryn to absorb me," I told Paul. "So get ready to leave soon. If I'm out, you will be too. There's going to be a big blowup when I tell her. I know exactly how Kathryn operates."

During his four years of working for Kathryn, Paul had booked concerts and set up meetings for me when Kathryn didn't need me. I asked Paul to continue to set up concerts so I would have work and an income after I quit.

After talking to Paul, I talked to God, wanting to be sure I wasn't making a mistake. "Is this what You want me to do, God? If You want me to stay, show me so I won't make a mistake." I had already prayed that way for weeks. Even though God didn't speak to me specifically, I feel that remaining with Kathryn indefinitely was not God's will.

A week after my announcement to Paul, I arrived at the CBS studio for a taping. Kathryn had already hired another pianist to replace me. Without saying a word, I watched the taping but said nothing. In one way it was a relief. At the same time, I felt hurt that she'd go ahead and hire him without telling me what she was going to do. I pushed those thoughts aside. I didn't want my job back, so I certainly wouldn't bring up the issue.

I waited around until they finished taping and everyone else had gone. "Kathryn, I'd like to talk to you for a minute." She came over to the edge of the stage where I was standing.

Although I wanted to comment about my replacement—and he was good—I decided to stick to the one subject I really wanted to talk about. Struggling to find the right words, I suddenly realized that it wouldn't have mattered how I told her; the reaction would have been the same.

"Kathryn, I want to get married," I said.

"To the Playboy bunny?" she snapped.

"I love her, Kathryn, I really do," I answered. "Besides that I want my own family, my own life. I'll still play for you, Kathryn. I'd like to work for you, but it isn't going to be my whole life."

"Dino," she said in a surprisingly controlled voice, "you're making a big mistake. A very big mistake. You have a wonderful ministry and you're going to ruin it by marrying her."

"I'm not asking for your permission," I said firmly. "I just wanted to tell you that I'm going to get married."

"You can't do that, Dino. You're not ready for such a serious, serious step. Oh, Dino, you will ruin your entire life."

"Kathryn, you've been good to me and I appreciate everything you've done for me," I said calmly. "But I have my own life. I'm going to marry Debby Keener."

"What about all those beautiful things I was going to leave you? You'll never get all those things I planned to leave you."

"I'm not interesting in your things," I said. "I want to go out and make my own way." I leaned forward and kissed her cheek. "Good-bye and thanks for everything."

"You're making a terrible, terrible mistake," she said as I walked away.

A few days later Kathryn went to see my parents because she thought she could convince my mother to use her influence to talk me out of marrying Debby. No matter how much pressure Kathryn exerted, she was wasting her time. Although she never said so, I'm sure my mother considered Kathryn possessive and knew she wanted to prevent my getting married.

"Helen," Kathryn said to my mother, "I came to see you because I'm concerned about Dino."

"Is he in trouble?" Mom asked.

"Yes, oh, yes, he is," she said. "You know about . . . about his plans?"

"I know about some of them," she said. "Dino talks to us a lot."

"He's making a big mistake," Kathryn said. "If only he would realize that this could ruin his entire life." She went on and on, tears in her eyes, explaining to my mother how it hurt her to see me throwing away my life.

Mom listened to Kathryn for a couple of hours, hearing the stories of Debby's past. Kathryn probably didn't realize that Debby and I had already prepared my family for the gossip.

"So you see, don't you? He just can't do this. We have to do something."

"It's his life," Mom said finally. "If he loves her and she loves him and they want to get married, then they have my blessing."

"But it's so wrong," Kathryn persisted, unable to accept that Mom had not been persuaded.

"This is for him to figure out," Mom answered wisely.

As I expected, the week I quit, Kathryn told Paul she didn't need his services any longer. She cut him off before he was able to find another position, which struck a heavy financial blow to him and his wife and six children. Although Paul had generated some additional income by booking concerts for me, it wasn't enough for him to live on.

A few months later, a close associate of Kathryn's cut off the monthly support for my Aunt Angie and Uncle Joe De Julio in Greece.

That decision severed the final link between Kathryn and me.

Chapter 14

AFTER KATHRYN

When I walked out of the CBS studio that February after-noon of 1975, I walked away from Kathryn Kuhlman and seven years of close work. I was sad because of the circumstances, but I was ready to begin my new life.

In May, Debby Keener and I were married in Sacramento. Her former youth pastor and my friend, Warren Grant, performed the ceremony. The late crooner, Dick Haymes, sang "Eternal Love" at our wedding. Everything went smoothly. It was a splendid beginning as we pledged to spend our lives together.

We sent Kathryn an invitation to the wedding but she didn't come. As a matter of fact, a day or so after receiving our invitation, she scheduled a service at the Shrine Auditorium for the day of our wedding. And we later heard that at the service, she made no mention of my wedding.

To my surprise, the media picked up the incident of my quitting and made a big thing of it. In his monologue of jokes on the "Tonight Show," Johnny Carson spoke about "Ex-aide betrays Kathryn Kuhlman."

Soon after the program aired, a reporter from the *National Enquirer* called, asking for information. "I quit," I told them. "Beyond that, I haven't anything more to tell you."

I ignored the press and refused to talk about Kathryn to anyone, even friends, because I didn't want to be quoted and misquoted. I hoped my silence would put an end to all the publicity and rumors. Also, despite all the articles that appeared, I wanted Kathryn to know that I wasn't out for revenge.

During the weeks following our split, I prayed constantly, "Dear God, please work this mess out. I'm willing to do whatever You want me to do. I know I have a ministry, and I felt I had to leave when I did." I threw myself on God's mercy and, most of the time, I was at peace.

The gossip about Debby continued and some of the carriers embellished it. One story said that she had a lengthy affair with Hugh Hefner.

"I thought God wiped away all past sins when people repented," I said to Debby. "Some of these folks just won't stop."

"Epecially Kathryn," Debby said. "She's acting more like a jilted lover than someone you worked for."

Some accused me of getting married on the rebound from leaving Kathryn's ministry as if she and I had been involved romantically and we suddenly broke up. I could never understand why people would think that way. Kathryn was close to seventy, and I was less than half her age. From my perspective, I was Kathryn's friend, a person concerned about her and her ministry.

Friends who knew of my desire to go out on my own thought I married Debby as an excuse to make the break. But as far as I was concerned, I married Debby because I loved her. Certainly along with my desire to get married was the strong determination to pull away from Kathryn. Debby brought an element of joy and laughter into my life that I needed. And I couldn't have made it through those few months after leaving Kathryn without her. When we heard the terrible stories being circulated, she would comfort and remind me, "Dino, *we* know the truth and so does God."

By getting married, I expected to begin a happy, carefree stage of life with my wife. But it wasn't always so easy. Being a concert pianist meant I had to travel constantly. In the beginning, Debby traveled with me, so we were never home.

Immediately after the breakup with Kathryn, I went on the road and held as many concerts as I could. I had previously booked engagements in a number of places. Deep in my heart I believed that my getting away from southern California would be the end of my problems with Kathryn because we were going separate ways. Breakups like this happened all the time.

I wanted to concentrate on my ministry. Yet we had a more difficult time than I had expected. Most of the churches that had booked us did so because they knew of me through Kathryn's ministry. Many of them canceled when they learned of the split.

I can still remember one pastor in Birmingham, Alabama, who didn't bother to ask me whether any of the stories were true. He picked up on a few rumors, accepted them as fact, and canceled with no explanation. When I received his letter of cancellation, I immediately phoned him. I was naive enough to think that he wanted to hear the truth. Just as foolishly, I assumed that if we talked, I could make him understand and we could work everything out. When he wouldn't speak with me by phone, I considered hopping a plane to Birmingham to talk with him, eyeball to eyeball. However, the more I considered it, I decided it wouldn't have made any difference, so why waste my time and money?

Cancellations continued. I would be booked to play at a church or an auditorium and, sometimes as late as the night before, a call would come: "We've decided to cancel." They had heard stories of some kind—either something horrible I had supposedly done to Kathryn or terrible stories about Debby's past. I finally was able to talk with one pastor who canceled.

"Why did you do this?" I asked.

"Because of the stories that are going around about you," he told me.

"What kind of stories?" I didn't want to defend anything he *hadn't* heard about.

"You know exactly what I mean," he said, "and I've been hearing them from reliable sources."

"What stories?" I persisted.

"About the way you betrayed Kathryn Kuhlman. You just up and left her when she needed you."

"That's not the way it happened," I said. "I'd like to explain . . ."

"Listen, Dino," he said. "I like you and appreciate your musical talent. But I like and respect Kathryn Kuhlman more, and I wouldn't want to do anything to hurt her."

"I'm not trying to hurt her," I said. "I just want to explain . . ."

"Let's forget it. People in the congregation have heard these stories too. I think it's better for everyone concerned if we cancel and say nothing more."

"I would still like to explain," I said. "After that, if you still want to cancel . . ."

"I don't think I want to hear any more," he said. "It would just be your word against what reliable people have told me. No, let's just forget the whole thing."

Nobody, it seemed, wanted to listen. Nobody wanted to know if the stories were true. When I phoned, they would say they didn't want to discuss the matter. If their secretaries said they were out, I would leave my number but none of them returned my calls.

What hurt even more were the men and women I had admired and respected a long time who wouldn't make themselves available even to talk, and it finally became obvious they were avoiding me. I wondered if it was because they didn't want to know the truth.

Slowly, the reality sank in. Either I had to speak up and tell the world my side of the story or remain silent. If I remained silent, many would believe the lies and exaggerations. As I prayed about what to do, I realized that in order to combat the stories, I would have had to say unkind things about Kathryn. I didn't want to do that so I finally decided to keep silent.

Until now, I've refused to speak about what prompted my leaving or what happened afterward. A lot of stories have appeared in print about Kathryn, many of them unkind and most of them untrue.

In his book, *Daughter of Destiny,* James Buckingham filled a chapter with ugly remarks about me. He insisted that I betrayed her by leaving, that I had left, "slinging mud." In the same book he stated that I rattled my saber against her. Nothing could be farther from the truth, not to mention that this author never verified his own statements. More than one friend suggested a lawsuit, but I didn't believe that was the right thing to do.

Buckingham never interviewed me. For material in his book that related to me, he accepted a third party's word that Kathryn had fired me, that I was vindictive, that I was spreading stories and shameful rumors about Kathryn. That third party had only recently come into Kathryn's life and, to my knowledge, was never someone she confided in or felt close to.

Despite the problems with cancellations, I did at least a hundred concerts a year. At first Debby traveled with me, but that soon got old for her, moving in and out of hotels, traveling to a new place virtually every day, sleeping in five different beds in a week's time. The first difficulties rose between us; however, I assumed we would eventually work through them.

From a positive perspective, I began to record with Light Records Company, owned by Ralph Carmichael. At that time, many considered them the leading contemporary gospel music company. So it pleased me that they were willing to take me on. I also had a number of bookings lined up that didn't fall through, so Debby and I drove across the country, creating additional bookings.

When I first started on my own, I hired a sound man named Gary Kitto, who was just out of Central Bible College. Gary helped me set up concerts by calling ahead when we were on the road. I was creating a new career while traveling from city to city.

One day, unexpectedly, Warren Grant, the man who performed our wedding ceremony, reappeared in my life. I'll never forget his words when he first contacted me: "Keep playing, Dino. Don't give up."

"It's not so much giving up," I said. "I'm struggling to find the right way to line up contacts." Then I told him what had been happening—how several pastors had canceled scheduled concerts.

"Brother, when one door closes, another opens," he said with a big smile on his face. Infused with energy, this tall, thin man always spoke positively. After spending five minutes with him, my spirits had lifted.

One of the first to stand behind us, Warren helped me to make contacts by calling on his friends. He encouraged me at every turn, and I'll always be grateful to him.

Warren was a close friend of Tom Zimmerman, the general superintendent of the Assemblies of God. One day Warren called Tom and told him the truth about the things that had really been going on with me. A few weeks later, Warren set up an appointment for Debby and me to visit the headquarters of the Assemblies of God in Springfield, Missouri.

"Dino, good to see you!" he said, looking genuinely pleased. He escorted us into his office, put his arm around my shoulder, and said, "Listen, Dino, we love you. I remember you from the days when Marie Brown was your pastor. She loved you, and she always told me to help you in any way I could. Now I've got that chance."

I don't suppose Tom Zimmerman had any idea how deeply I needed to hear his words. While talking to us, he said, "Gold needs to go through fire before it's refined. That's also true with you. In God's sight, you're much more precious than gold." So Tom also helped us. With the endorsements of Warren Grant and Tom Zimmerman, we had soon regained credibility in the Christian community.

Assuming that everything that had to do with Kathryn Kuhlman now lay behind me, I concentrated on establishing a stable marriage. Debby and I didn't want any more problems. We wanted to be away from all the old pressures and turmoil. Filled with optimism, we reminded each other, "We're going to make it."

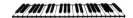

During the summer of 1975, we met another man who was to have a large role in my professional life over the next ten years. I played and taught a session in the summer at the annual Christian Artists Seminar in Estes Park, Colorado. On the second day Larry Sparks introduced himself and asked, "Would you be interested in having me as your booking agent?"

I knew Larry was part of Christian Artists in Los Angeles. A sharp guy in his midtwenties, he's what I would consider very California-looking: He was blond, tan, tall, and thin, and had an energetic personality.

"I'll think about it," I said. I hesitated because I was barely making it financially, and my pride wouldn't let me tell him how bad things were.

"I think I understand the situation," Larry said, "with your leaving Kathryn Kuhlman."

"It's been a little tough," I told him vaguely.

"But that doesn't have to work against you," he said.

"I don't see how I can make it any different." I told him about the cancellations.

"Dino, look at it this way. A lot of questions are being raised. People ask, who is Dino? What's he really like? They've heard the gossip and are intrigued by it all. Why not take advantage of it instead of running away? Rather than being a liability, your name and former association with Kathryn could get you into a number of places. And from there, your keyboard ability will do the rest."

"That might work," I said skeptically.

"You see, Dino, Kathryn built you up as this aloof person—this unapproachable Dino in the flashy clothes," Larry persisted. "I can market you. Since people want to know who you really are, here's your chance!"

"I'm just not sure," I hesitated, still not convinced.

Finally, I arranged for him to visit our home a few weeks later. He stayed overnight at my parents' home.

When we met the next day, Larry Sparks said clearly, "I'd like to work with you. I've admired your piano work for a long time, and I know there's a market out there for you. Because of your image, a lot of curious people want to know what happened between you and Kathryn."

"I'm not sure that's the thing to do," I said.

"Look, Dino," he said, "I can only get you booked. Then you deliver the goods or that's the end of it. I know I could get you good bookings."

"But what about the stories going around?"

"You wouldn't have to talk about Kathryn," he said. "You wouldn't have to say anything. Just play."

"It's still going to be tough to book you in some places because of the Kathryn Kuhlman thing," Larry admitted. "And you'll be facing two kinds of people at your concerts. First, those who come out of curiosity. No problem there. But you'll also face those who'll want to turn you off because of their loyalty to Kathryn. But, not to worry, Dino, we'll overcome that as well."

"We don't have anything to lose," I said. Debby and I had been booking my concerts, calling pastors, friends, and acquaintances we had made over the years. Larry was positive about everything and had already established a reputation as a guy who made things happen. Finally, he persuaded me.

A few minutes later, we said good-bye, and he drove on to my parents' place.

Larry later told me that he couldn't sleep that night—he couldn't shut off his mind. As he prayed, he felt God was guiding him, giving him ideas on how to market me. After a couple of hours of tossing in bed, Larry decided to get in his car and drive down Beach Boulevard. He figured he would drive to the beach, park his car, and find a secluded spot where he could pray and meditate about this.

I didn't know it at the time, but Larry has multiple sclerosis. Although it hasn't slowed him down much, he does have some problems with his coordination. As he drove down Beach Boulevard at 1:30 that morning, he apparently was weaving slightly. A police car came alongside and pulled him over. At that time of morning, the police weren't used to encountering anyone looking for a place to pray. "Where's your license, buddy?" The patrolman took his license, returned to the patrol car, and punched the information into his computer.

"I've got to lock you up," the patrolman said when he returned to Larry's car. He put handcuffs on a protesting Larry, drove him to the station, and booked him.

Just after 4:00 A.M., the telephone rang and I grabbed it.

"Hello, Dino. This is Larry."

"Yeah," I mumbled, wondering why he was calling at that hour.

"You won't believe this, but I'm in jail in Huntington Beach. Can you come and bail me out? I need $360 in cash. They won't take a check or a credit card. It has to be cash, which is why I'm calling you."

Is he on drugs? Is God warning me about this guy? I wondered.

"I feel like a jerk," he said. "I'm sorry to bother you, but I don't know anybody else in the area."

The earnestness in his voice convinced me.

"Why are you in jail?"

"A traffic ticket. I mean, an old one that I forgot about. I only have about a hundred dollars with me, so I can't pay my bail."

"I don't have that kind of cash here," I said, "but I'll do what I can."

Debby and I searched the house for money, but we could find only $112. We woke up our neighbors next door and borrowed $53. Then I called my parents, and they had a hundred. I collected the money and drove to the police station.

A dejected Larry sat next to two men who were either winos or on drugs in a corner of a dark, filthy cell. Larry was so embarrassed he could hardly look at me.

"I'm sorry, Dino," he said as we walked out of the police station. It was the fourth time he had said that.

"Hey, tell you what," I said, "I've still got enough money left for coffee and doughnuts. Let's get some and forget about your night in jail."

That was my introduction to Larry Sparks and the beginning of a professional and personal friendship. And right then I needed all the friends I could get.

Chapter 15

A SAD DEATH

"... died yesterday ... complications from surgery ..."

Sitting in the Albuquerque hotel and trying to unwind after a concert, I turned on the television news. For several minutes I had only been half-listening until the announcer said her name again—"Kathryn Kuhlman." I snapped to full attention. As I stared at the screen, the station showed a clip from a Kathryn Kuhlman service at Los Angeles' Shrine Auditorium.

"Debby, quick! Come here!" I yelled to my wife in the bathroom. "Listen to this!"

A terrible pain started gnawing inside me as I stared at the screen and listened to the reporter review her recent medical history. I had known of Kathryn's heart surgery two weeks earlier—the media had blared the story of the woman healer who herself needed healing. All the reports indicated that she was improving after the repair of her mitral valve.

"Kathryn died," I managed to say when my wife came into the room. I pointed to the clip showing Kathryn, dressed in a flowing white chiffon gown, standing on the platform, her arms raised, the footlights accentuating the redness of her hair and making it resemble a golden halo. I stared at her radiant smile. That was the Kathryn I knew; that was the Kathryn I loved.

Abruptly the station switched to a commercial, but in my mind, I was still seeing Kathryn as she stood before that large crowd. More than once she had spoken of pouring out her life for the gospel; now I understood what she meant.

I don't recall what my wife said, if anything, I had gone into shock. Some people seemed indestructible, and Kathryn was one of them. Although she had spoken to me several times of how she imagined her death would be, I never dwelt much on the subject. As a matter of fact, we had even talked, on occasion, of how we both might still be alive when Jesus Christ returned. So now I didn't want to believe what I had just heard.

Kathryn Kuhlman—this extraordinary woman, this powerful personality, this international figure, this great lady with whom I had worked for several years—was dead. I tried to deny the news.

She couldn't have died. Not Kathryn.

But she *was* dead.

For the rest of the day memories of some of the special times we had shared swept over me: our travels, our working together, our planning of services. I remembered quiet talks at her beautiful house or meals we shared in a restaurant the day after a big meeting. I recalled the first time I had appeared on her television show and the immediate rapport we had with one another. Sadly, I also remembered other times—the bad times, the disagreements, the occasions when harsh and angry words passed between us, especially near the end of our working side by side.

I buried my face in my hands and wept. Kathryn Kuhlman had been a powerful force in my life—at times too powerful. But she had also done so much for me. Above all, we had been friends—really good friends. I felt as if a member of my immediate family had died.

I can still visualize Kathryn today, as she stood on the edge of the platform, dramatically reaching out, opening her heart and ministering to people. No matter how old she was, she possessed a dynamism and what I call a special gift from God. Night after night she spoke to audiences and told them, "I can't help you but there is someone who can. His name is Jesus! Ah, yes! Jesus is the only help you need!"

Kathryn was known by millions as a faith healer and evangelist. But she was more than that.

Born in Missouri, Kathryn had little education and no formal training as a preacher, yet she had that presence about her—a kind of sacred aura—that in my experience, few people have come close to equaling and none surpassing. In 1947, when she was in her early forties, she emerged in the Pittsburgh area as a healing evangelist (although she hated being called a healer, always insisting that God did the healing). Before she died, millions recognized her face, her emphatic voice, and dramatic gestures; yet Kathryn remained a woman whom few people really knew. Although she accepted herself as a public figure, she always protected her privacy.

Despite what had happened at the end of our relationship, I never stopped admiring Kathryn or recognizing her unique spiritual ability.

After I left her ministry, many changes took place in Kathryn's life. She became involved with a new crowd. They persuaded her to fly in their private plane and traveled everywhere with her.

My theory is that, already in deteriorating health and not having the strength to fight, Kathryn allowed these strangers to monopolize her. She lost touch with her former friends, and the new crowd virtually took control of her life. Whatever their reasons, they always wanted Kathryn close to them. They monopolized her time and, eventually, everything else in her life until she was totally dependent upon them.

For years, doctors had warned Kathryn of her heart condition. Yet she seldom complained, and few of us close to her realized the seriousness of her condition until the fall of 1975. By September, Kathryn couldn't hide anymore. Any close observer could tell she was a sick woman.

In November 1975 Kathryn had a heart attack while staying at the Century Plaza Hotel in Los Angeles. Tink and Sue Wilkerson, who had become close friends with Kathryn shortly after I left the ministry, rushed her to St. John's Hospital. Right after Christmas, the Wilkersons flew Kathryn to the Hillcrest Medical Center in Tulsa.

Oral and Evelyn Roberts visited and were able to see her. Evelyn later told me, "Kathryn gave up. She willed to die."

Kathryn died apart from her friends, apart from those who had known and worked for her. It seemed that the only people with her at her death were the Wilkersons. In her last year, the Wilkersons had frequently traveled with Kathryn, and in her last days, they had remained close to her, protecting her not only from unwanted media but also from friends. I knew of several who weren't able to get in to see Kathryn—friends from the years and employees who idolized her. Even Maggie Hartner, who flew all the way from Pittsburgh to see Kathryn, was unable to visit her.

Just before she died, Kathryn wrote a new will, which sparked a major controversy after her death. Some believed that Maggie Hartner had been the major beneficiary of the first will, but we heard later that the Wilkersons had instead received the major portion of her estate.

I found out that the funeral was going to be held at Forest Lawn Memorial Park, Glendale, California. I wanted to go but it was a closed funeral, with only a select few in attendance. I knew that with the Wilkersons in charge, I wouldn't be allowed. I sent flowers as my last tribute to a great and wonderful lady.

I brooded on the day of Kathryn's funeral, wondering what had gone on in Kathryn's heart in those last days. If she had any thoughts of me, I'm sure they were that I had let her down, that I had no further concern for her ministry. I honestly don't think she ever understood my position.

My biggest regret was that we wouldn't have the chance to settle things between us. Kathryn had been a powerful and godly influence in my life. I had hoped that one day we could get all of that taken care of between us and that she would know the real truth.

"It's so sad," I said, "that she died without my having talked to her one more time." It was a sad death.

All through the day, my thoughts kept returning to her. Kathryn Kuhlman had chosen me to be not only an employee but one of those rare individuals who spent time with her in private, who traveled many places with her, who visited her home often, who knew her lifestyle well. And I think I'm also one of the few people who understood her.

Until her death, I held on to the hope that one day we would resolve our differences and perhaps work together again. But I never saw her after I quit.

My mind wandered to the last personal report I had received of Kathryn before her hospitalization. When I resigned in February, she was preparing for a service in Las Vegas in May. Had I stayed, I would have played the piano for her.

In May, a few days before leaving for Vegas, Kathryn drove from her home in Newport Beach to my parents' house in Huntington Beach. Naturally they invited her inside and treated her nicely because they loved her too. They had heard the things she had said after I left, but they never hated her. I think they understood her loneliness and sadness and had genuinely liked her.

When Kathryn arrived she was on the verge of tears. Mom later said that she had never seen Kathryn so downcast. The two women talked a long time. My name came up often but not once did Kathryn ever mention my leaving, my marriage, or my wife, although by then I had been married for two months.

Before she left, Kathryn gave way to her tears. "What has happened shouldn't happen between families," she said, "and you're my family. You'll always be part of my family. Despite what's happened, I want to see you people. Please, don't let anything sever our relationship.

At one point, still crying heavily, she said to my parents, "I would like to have Dino come to Las Vegas." She didn't ask me directly; nor did she ask my folks to invite me. Kathryn knew that my parents would tell me everything that she had said. Had that incident happened before I was married, just her wanting me to play would have been enough for me to get on the phone and tell her, "Kathryn, I'd love to play for you in Vegas."

Yet I had brought about the separation because I *needed* to be away from her influence and to take charge of my own life. Had I played, we would have ended up in the same situation where we had been months earlier. My quitting would then have had no significance.

Perhaps in recounting this incident of Kathryn visiting my family, it sounds as if I'm accusing her of playing games. I'm not. She gave me an emotional response. She did miss me, and I'm convinced she loved my family and had a close relationship to my grandmother. Despite my leaving and all the painful words between us, however, I think she very much wanted to have me with her in Vegas.

Through the years, I've thought often of writing an open letter entitled *Dear Kathryn,* to tell the world and Kathryn how I felt. And I finally did.

Dear Kathryn,

This is a letter I've wanted to write to you for a long, long time to say the things I was never able to say to you. I've held this within me, and now I'm determined to express through this letter how much you've meant to me and how much you have influenced my life and ministry. I wanted to see you, to tell you how I felt when you were lying in the hospital. In those dark days, you must have known that you were dying. As I heard medical reports over television, I didn't want to believe it could happen to you.

I was barred from coming to see you at the hospital. I don't know if you knew this. Several of us who truly loved you weren't able to be there at your side. And that's one of the biggest regrets I have. But at last I'm getting the opportunity to say these things to you.

Dear Kathryn, you've been a major influence on my life. By your own example, far more than by what you said, you taught me how God can mightily use individuals who totally commit themselves to him.

The other day a man who had been a faithful follower of yours approached me after a concert. "Dino, I feel that same power and anointing in your music that I have felt in our beloved Kathryn's life and ministry." He didn't know it, but he couldn't have said anything more wonderful to me.

Since you died, many Kathryn Kuhlman clones have come on the scene. I've said, as I'm sure many of your thousands of followers have said, this can't be. There was only one Kathryn.

Please forgive me for my part in the misunderstanding between us and our sad parting. It has been fourteen years since you left this world and I'm fourteen years older and, I hope wiser and less rambunctious.

Sometimes, especially when I start getting discouraged, I think of you up there watching me. If you can see what's going on in my life, I hope you're pleased.

And finally, Kathryn, you used to say, "When I see the Lord, all I'm going to say is, 'I've tried.'" When I meet God, I also want to look at Him and say, "I've tried."

*With love forever,
Your friend,*

Dino

The day after Kathryn's funeral my flowers were returned. Across the address was scrawled one word: *Refused.*

Yes, it was a sad death.

Chapter 16

ANOTHER ENDING

After Kathryn's death and as I traveled more widely, I encountered a strange obsession—the cloning of Kathryn. Beginning in late 1976 a number of Kuhlman clones started popping up around the country. I met a few of them—all trying to imitate her style. They tell me that this happens when famous people die, like the widespread imitation of Elvis Presley. Whatever their reasons, it troubled me when I saw the cloning of Kathryn.

Paul signed a contract for me to play at a place called the Shekinah Fellowship in Long Beach, California. When I got there, I didn't meet the preacher although I saw him at a distance. He was about twenty years old, tall, slim, and handsome.

As I looked around, the first shock came. This preacher had the place set up so that it looked like the Shrine Auditorium in Los Angeles where Kathryn regularly had held her meetings.

When the service began, the choir sang Kathryn's theme songs "Nothing Is Impossible" and "He Touched Me." Using the same arrangements and phrasing, the choir even sounded like Kathryn's old choir.

This is spooky, I thought. As I looked around and listened, everything at the meeting seemed to progress exactly like one of Kathryn's services. It was all set up as if Kathryn would soon walk across the platform to preach and heal.

"Who is this guy?" I asked Paul, who had gone with me.

He told me the preacher's name, but that wasn't what I meant. It was as if he had gone to an unlimited amount of research to find out everything about Kathryn and then had set about to duplicate it.

I didn't hear the preacher speak until he introduced me to the audience. As I listened to him, he sounded as if he were the embodiment of Kuhlman—the same voice and doing her gestures with the same precision.

"Can you believe this?" In a state of shock, I turned to Paul. "I'm not walking out on that stage. This guy is trying to make it look like I'm his pianist."

Paul whispered, "We signed a contract, Dino."

Paul was right and I couldn't back out. The man imitated Kathryn perfectly as he gestured my way. "Here's Dino at the piano."

"Go on," Paul said as he pushed me out on stage.

The preacher wore black pants and a shirt with frilly, puffy sleeves—as close to a blouse as a man's shirt could get. But more than that, he was doing all of Kathryn's movements to perfection. It was as if he had practiced his act for hours.

Momentarily I stared at the audience—mostly young people. They had come to worship and to receive from God. But I was in a terrible state of mind. Instead of going directly to the piano as I had normally done with Kathryn, I walked over to the microphone. "For one second," I said, "I thought I was in one of Kathryn Kuhlman's services."

The audience laughed faintly and I realized I had no right to take out my anger and frustration on them. Just at that moment, I glanced at the preacher. He stood several feet away, and even then his posture was a complete (and perfect) imitation.

"I didn't think that for one second," he said, still using her way of speaking, "I didn't think I was Kathryn Kuhlman for one second."

I bet, I thought to myself. I suspect my face showed how I felt. At the same time, I realized I wasn't in a very spiritual mood, so I turned and went to the piano bench.

My professionalism and training enabled me to play. Even then it was a strange experience and I played automatically, going through two or three numbers, not looking at the man and not wanting to see him desecrate the memory of a holy woman.

As soon as I finished, I got up from the piano bench, bowed and then headed for the wings. I practically ran out of that auditorium. Anger, frustration, and pain all boiled inside. I kept thinking, this lady was so special, so gifted, and all of your imitating is still just imitation. You'll never have the real thing she had.

Oddly enough, it was only after Kathryn's prominence that other evangelists, and especially those on television, began to call out healings and miracles as she had done. This didn't bother me as much as Kathryn actually being imitated. I thought they were just picking up on something that worked for her. Maybe it would also work for them.

I'm not saying God can't use others or that by doing things the way Kathryn did wasn't accurate, but I had worked with the queen of faith healers and, in my opinion, other than Oral Roberts, none of them ever seemed to have the same kind of gift that she did.

Debby and I were still newlyweds in 1976, and we spent most of our time trying to adjust to our life together. New churches opened their doors to us, and we were able to do more than a hundred concerts the first year. But being constantly on the road was difficult. We slept in a different bed every night and often traveled ten hours at a time for the next concert. The Kathryn Kuhlman business popped up just about every place we went. For those who had heard of me, my name still meant "Kathryn Kuhlman's piano player."

Another issue surfaced fairly early in our marriage. After a few weeks of traveling with me and staying in the background, Debby finally spoke up. "Dino," she said, "I'd like to sing one or two songs in your next concert. I want to be a part of what's going on."

It seemed natural for Debby to want to be a vital part of my ministry. And I reasoned that learning together the hassles of this business firsthand would make our marriage stronger. I admired my wife for what she wanted to do.

Debby, being career-minded and assertive, thought differently than I did about my work. I saw it as ministry first and then as entertainment. While I wanted her as part of my professional life, I felt she pushed too hard and too fast.

"Give it time," I'd say to her. "Let's go at this slowly and see where you fit in best."

Maybe I didn't say those words right because an argument soon started. "You don't like the way I sing, do you?"

"Of course I do—"

"Then why are you holding back? Let me sing with you."

"This is a ministry *and* entertainment. We need to be sure of God's will in this."

The Kuhlman matter had also affected her. Debby didn't need to prove anything to me, but maybe she needed to prove something to herself—and to others, especially those who had criticized her and gossiped about her. I wonder if she was saying to the world, "See, I am all right! Dino married the right person. I have a valid ministry too!"

From my perspective, Debby tried too hard and didn't know when to stop trying. Debby reveled in her opportunities to sing; however, I soon detected something else happening. I noticed a spirit of competition edging in between us. After a short period of singing a couple of numbers, she wanted more time on the program. While I didn't feel competitive toward her, I sensed that she worked hard to prove that she was as good as or better than I.

With inner reluctance, I gave in. Before the year ended, she had insisted upon and received equal billing. We soon had the Dino and Debby show. My marriage was important—the most important aspect of my life. Since sharing the spotlight seemed crucial to Debby, I wouldn't have fought it; I had committed myself to making our marriage survive.

Our relationship never went smoothly, however. We had arguments from the first week of our marriage, and, unfortunately, they became more frequent. At first we argued primarily about professional matters—how to do things in concerts. But soon we began to disagree about personal issues.

Whenever possible, I tried to avoid argument because I'm not as articulate as Debby: I didn't stand a chance against Debby. I'm one of those people who figures out bright things to say long after the conversation has ended, whereas Debby could let the words fly without any apparent effort.

Most of the time I went along with whatever Debby wanted. *We'll get used to each other,* I'd tell myself. I thought that as people accepted me and my ministry and as the Kathryn Kuhlman trouble receded, Debby would let up and wouldn't need to work so compulsively.

Then good news came for us: Debby and I were going to have a baby. The news made us ecstatic, and Debby began planning for the future. Those days became some of the happiest times of our marriage. We decided to buy our own house and had fun checking out places to live. We finally decided on a place in Santa Ana.

On January 14, 1977, God gave us a beautiful baby girl. We named her Christina (after YaYa) Ellen (after my mother whose Greek name is Eleni). Except for being on the road for periods of time, we tried to live like normal people. Debby and Christina traveled with me for a year. And though it was wonderful for me to have them along, it laid a heavier burden on Debby.

I wanted our marriage to work, yet all along a link was missing: unity—we never had it. Emotional flare-ups seemed more normal than peace; friction existed between us over just about everything.

When it came to my concerts and television shows, Debby had strong opinions on how I ought to do things. But because I knew what I was doing and believed I did my concerts well, I started to resist.

For several weeks I had been getting closer to admitting to myself that her being part of the program just wasn't working for either of us. Debby wasn't happy and she kept getting sick—a touch of the flu, a nagging backache, a pinched nerve.

One night after we had come home to Santa Ana for a few days, I approached Debby. "Maybe you should stay home instead of traveling with me," I said. I had prepared myself for a verbal attack and I wasn't disappointed.

"You don't want me on your program anymore, do you?" she responded.

"I think you'll be happier and feel a lot better with the pressure off you. And besides, I can't take the arguing all the time. I know what God wants me to do and I'm going to continue with my concerts—"

"You don't love me," she said. "I know you don't love me."

"Of course, I love you—"

"No, you don't! If you really loved me, you'd want me at your side all the time. If you loved me, you'd insist on spending more time with me."

No matter how hard I tried to explain, Debby insisted that I didn't love her. Suddenly, the argument took a turn.

"Another thing," Debby paused. "You slept with Kathryn, Dino, didn't you?"

"Of course not. I can't believe you'd even think such a thing."

"I think you did," she said. "So why don't you tell me about it?"

"There's nothing to tell, because nothing ever happened."

"I don't believe that."

The bickering continued for most of the evening. As I've already said, I was never a match for Debby when it came to using words. I didn't have her flow of words. But as our talk came to a close, I remained firm about doing the concerts alone.

"This is the way I have to do it," I said. On this I remained adamant, and she finally accepted it. I was returning to the format I had started with—without Debby's singing.

My decision was probably the beginning of the end.

But first, another heartache came.

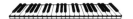

"It's YaYa," Mom said on the phone, early one morning in 1977. "She's had a stroke." Mom broke down and cried.

"How bad?"

"She's in the hospital. Your Aunt Angie was with her when it happened."

Mom was preparing to fly back to New York to be at YaYa's hospital bedside. She filled in as many details as she knew then.

Joe and Angie De Julio, home from Greece, were staying with YaYa. She left them and went shopping. When she finished, she walked up the five flights of stairs to her apartment. In the kitchen, she started taking fruit out of her shopping bag and fell. The De Julios ran into the kitchen and saw her. Immediately, they called an ambulance.

YaYa had had a massive stroke, leaving her entire left side paralyzed. Mom stayed with YaYa around the clock until the doctors released her. Then she brought YaYa to California.

"My mother isn't going into a nursing home," she said. "As long as I can take care of her, this is where she stays."

And YaYa stayed with my parents. I visited her as much as I could. She couldn't really talk, though she tried. She kept saying the Greek word for *now,* over and over in a kind of rapid-fire pattern. We didn't know if she understood what was going on or not. But I think she did. When I'd sit down and talk to YaYa, her eyes would follow mine, and when I'd tell her something pleasant, her eyes would light up. I just knew she understood.

Having my grandmother an invalid was hard on Mom. YaYa was a heavy woman, so Mom had trouble lifting her and doing everything for her. But Mom never complained. "This is the way I want it," she said.

For two years Mom and Dad took care of YaYa, night and day. We had known from the time they brought her to California that it would not be long before she would die. But we loved YaYa so much that we just couldn't think of letting her go.

Then, one night, YaYa gently slipped away. When she died, I felt I had lost a part of my life. She was the greatest prayer warrior in my life and had always been there when I needed her. Now she was gone. In my grief, I cried out to the Lord.

"Oh, God, how will I get by without her advice, her loving encouragement, and especially without knowing she's praying for me?" I fell deeper into sorrow, until suddenly a thought filled my mind and lifted my soul.

Her prayers are still with me, I thought.

And I knew they were.

Chapter 17

SPEAKING OUT

Within a year after Kathryn's death, two biographies about Kathryn appeared on the Christian booksellers' listings. Kathryn had intended to select someone to write her biography, but, to my knowledge, she never made a choice. I think she kept putting it off because she didn't believe she would die. Despite her chronic heart condition, I honestly believe she expected to live until Jesus Christ returned. Since she didn't view her death as an imminent matter, getting her biography written posed no major decision for her.

Logos International (which no longer exists) rushed out *Daughter of Destiny* by Jamie Buckingham. Although Jamie Buckingham had previously ghostwritten several of her books, Kathryn said to me, "I don't want Jamie Buckingham to write that book." She was quite firm about it; I recall the incident quite plainly. We were in her Grandville condo in Newport Beach in the summer of 1973 when she said, "He thinks he knows me but he doesn't."

I hurt deeply when I read the book, and I resented the things Buckingham wrote about me. The chapter entitled "Betrayed" painted the worst possible picture of me. It all but blamed me for her death. Despite the fact that he claimed he tried to interview me, Buckingham wrote me one letter.

After the release of Buckingham's book, most of Kathryn's friends assumed that I was down on her. Other than from this book, I have no idea where they got such tales. Not once did I ever publicly speak against Kathryn Kuhlman.

Buckingham's book could easily tarnish the memories people had of Kathryn. He made statements that seemed to question her moral character. If she had been alive when the book came out, I know she would have been hurt. So part of my purpose in writing this book is to tell Kathryn and her friends how I truly felt about the situation.

Three or four years after the book's publication, I started appearing on TV shows. More than one host said to me privately, "I had heard you knew Kathryn Kuhlman well. Tell us what she was like."

"Kathryn was a wonderful, gifted woman," I usually said. "She had a ministry like no one I've ever seen before. God used her to change lives, and people were healed all the time."

Most of the hosts seemed surprised at my positive answer. I told them I would not talk about Kathryn, and they respected my silence.

When I was going through some tough times, not many came to me out of kindness or concern. But a few said, "We're praying for you. We don't want to know the details." I'll always be grateful to those loving, compassionate individuals.

In late 1979, Jim Bakker phoned from Charlotte, North Carolina, where he hosted "PTL" on television. I'd first met the Bakkers shortly after I began to work for Kathryn, and they had featured me on "PTL" several times. Even after Kathryn's death, the Bakkers asked me to play. Despite all the scandal that came later, my experiences with Jim and

Tammy were always uplifting. And I'm grateful because they were available to me when I needed caring people.

"Tammy and I would like to have you appear on 'PTL'," he said. "But, Dino, I think it's time you talked about Kathryn. I'd like you to have the chance to open up about what really did happen and to express your feelings about her."

"I don't know if I'm ready to talk about it," I said.

"Let me tell you this much, then," he said. "I'm going to have another guest on the show."

"Oh? Who?"

"Jamie Buckingham," he answered. "And I'm going to ask him about Kathryn and about you. Dino, this may be the time to get out there and let people know the whole truth."

"Okay," I said. "Let's do the show."

Just before going on the show, I prayed as I had been praying for days: "God, help me be nice." Not only had many of Buckingham's statements hurt, but a lot of hostility had built up inside me toward the writer, even though I didn't want it to. My natural instinct was to jab Jamie at a dozen vulnerable points. But I knew that wouldn't honor God and would only cause more accusations and pain. "God, guide me when I open my mouth," I said as I faced the audience of Jim Bakker's talk show.

On the day of the taping before a live audience, the Bakkers kept Buckingham and me in separate rooms so that we couldn't see each other. Jamie went on first. Jim hadn't told him I was going to be on the show.

"We want you to tell us about Kathryn Kuhlman," he said, "and we have someone else here who was closely associated with her." Jim paused and called my name while the audience applauded. Jamie's face reddened, but he greeted me when I appeared.

I'd always admired Jim's ability as a talk-show host, and he was never better than that day. He handled the discussion smoothly and treated us both courteously as he questioned us.

After informing the audience about Kathryn Kuhlman's ministry and her death, Jim Bakker turned to me. "Dino, here's Jamie Buckingham. What would you like to say to him?"

Suddenly, I no longer felt angry. I think I was nice to him in everything I said. And at one point, I leaned toward him and said, "Jamie, I think Kathryn was one of the most wonderful women I've ever known." From the surprised expression on his face, I think he had expected me to put her down. He had written so critically of me and my behavior that I'm sure he believed I was against Kathryn.

I told Jamie and the audience that I loved Kathryn, that God had used her life mightily, and that people had been saved and healed through her work. I told him I was sorry that he had written what he did in his book, not just about me, but about Kathryn. He seemed embarrassed and I felt sorry for him. And I didn't really want to put him on the spot. Yet I had a few things I felt I needed to say.

Facing Jamie on national television, I also expressed my disappointment that he hadn't tried harder to get in touch with me and ask me about my role in the Kathryn Kuhlman incident. Specifically, I mentioned the chapter that he called "Betrayed." He had stated his information as fact, though he had only the information other people had told him.

Jamie defended himself and explained why he had written the book. He insisted that Kathryn had come to him and said, "If anybody writes my book, you are the person I want to write it because I trust you to say the right thing."

"No woman would have wanted those things written about her," I said, when he paused. "You wrote about her divorce and the flaws of her character and made a big thing about her not wanting to reveal her age. Parts of the book sounded like the *National Enquirer*. You pulled things from her past that I know Kathryn wouldn't have wanted written."

"I was trying to give a full picture of the woman—"

"But you brought out things that no one was talking about and made them conversational again. Kathryn died and your book didn't allow her to go out in glory so that people could remember the wonderful things about her. She never had a chance to defend herself."

"I'm sorry that it happened," he said, "but the book is out and it's after the fact now. This is how I felt and how the evidence appeared to me. . . ." He rambled on, but he did apologize on the show and I appreciated that.

As soon as the show went off the air, I received telephone calls from everywhere. But the call I most appreciated came from Rex and Maude Aimee Humbard. The Humbards had helped Kathryn years earlier in Akron, Ohio. And she, in turn, helped their ministry get started in Akron. They had remained friends for many years and Kathryn highly respected them. Because they thought that I didn't love Kathryn and had let her down when she needed me, they had held some bad feelings toward me. When they heard me speak up for Kathryn on the show, they immediately called to apologize.

From all over the country, people phoned to tell me how happy they were to hear me speak up and to set the record straight. Each of them told a story of the special place Kathryn held in their hearts. And I was able to say, "I feel the same way."

I'm thankful Jim Bakker set up that TV show. The timing was perfect for me to open up to the public and tell them how I felt about Kathryn. And I hoped that somehow, as I answered all those phone calls, Kathryn would be able to hear and would know how much I appreciated and admired her.

Debby and I continued to grow farther apart. She's people-oriented and *must* have people around her. With friends present, her spirits soared. Left alone, she sank into depressive moods.

In those low moods, she'd say things like, "You don't have any compassion. All you think about is yourself and your piano."

Or she would complain about my being on the road. "If you cared, you'd be with me more. You'd find a way to come home to Christina and me." When she was feeling down, her words had a real sting to them. Even though I knew she said things she didn't really mean, the words still hurt.

"I have to stay out there and work," I said. "That's my ministry. That's how I earn our income . . ."

"You could figure out ways to get home more often. Or get more money for each concert." She had a string of ideas, none of them practical or realistic.

When I first met Debby, her distinct attitude and personality attracted me. But her moods often swung from extreme highs to the pits. I needed the lightness, the fun, the relaxation, and the enjoyment of going to parties and being with people my own age.

By the end of 1978, Debby had agreed to stay in California while I was on the road. In the days that followed, our relationship changed. Debby continued to fill her life with people and activities. People easily opened up to her, and she thrived on that. "I can't just sit around home all day," she'd say.

And a person like Debby probably couldn't.

In 1979, I came home after a two-week tour in the Midwest. Before I said a word I could see that Debby was in one of her low moods.

"I don't love you. I want a divorce," she confronted me.

"We can't give up," I pleaded. "We've got to come to grips with this thing. Sure, we've got problems, but we can work them out."

"It's too late," she insisted. "I don't love you and I know you haven't loved me for a long time. I want a divorce."

"No way a divorce," I said flatly. "No way."

"I want a divorce and I'm going to get one." Another long spray of verbal bullets followed.

"I don't care what you say," I said. "I'm not going to grant you a divorce."

Moving closer, she stared with hostility right into my eyes. "If you don't, I'll go to our friends. I'll tell them about our problems—your not caring and your staying away all the time," she threatened.

She knew me too well. I've always had a strong sense of privacy, and I didn't want the world knowing about my family. I could just imagine where this would lead. If Debby started talking, not only friends, but the press, especially the sleaze tabloids, would grab hold of the information and could easily distort it. Christina was too young to be affected then, but it would haunt her later. I thought of my parents and didn't want Mom and Dad hurt. They'd already been through enough after my leaving Kathryn.

"I'll tell all our friends about you and Kathryn too."

"There's nothing to tell," I said wearily.

"You went to bed with her. Dino, I know you did."

I shook my head. "You know that's not true."

Debby was quick to shoot off harsh words of accusation in heated moments. I figured out that the crowd she traveled with before we married would have done things like that. Frequently when we got into arguments, she would say that she knew I hadn't told her the whole story about Kathryn and me. She wanted me to break down and confess that Kathryn and I had had an affair for years. But it wasn't true, and I wasn't going to satisfy her by confirming a lie as truth.

"And that's not all!" Her voice was rising, I could tell she was losing control. "I'm going to see the pastor. I'll tell him that you don't really love me, that you don't care anything about me."

"Think about Christina," I said. "For Christina's sake, let's work it out."

"I want a divorce! I want a divorce!"

"No! No! No!"

"I already have the papers!" she said. From her purse she pulled out the petition and shoved it into my hands. Seeing those papers threw me into shock. I knew she had been unhappy, but I was unprepared for the extent and intensity of what she had done.

"This is just too quick!" I protested.

"Not for me! I've been unhappy for a long time. For too long."

But I still refused to sign.

I never asked if there was anyone else. Maybe I was still too shocked. Probably more true, I didn't want to know if there was. However, from what mutual friends told me later, Keith Hefner, Hugh's brother, reappeared and swept Debby off her feet.

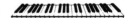

I moved back in with my parents. Debby went to an attorney for the separation papers. The legal agreement banned me from going into our house where she was still living with Christina. I didn't try to go inside, but occasionally, I'd get so lonely for Christina that I would drive up to the house, park in front, and watch, excited to catch a glimpse of my daughter.

I left for a ten-day tour shortly after Debby's and my separation. When I returned to my parents' home, I realized how much I missed my daughter. As I sat with my Dad in the living room, I shared my pain and he listened. Dad had become easy to talk to, and I felt he understood me.

Finally I said, "How about going over to the house? Just to look." Dad nodded and headed for the door.

We drove over to the house where Debby and I had lived for the past three years. When we arrived, I saw a moving van parked in front and movers loading the furniture. "Oh, no," I said. "Dad! She can't! She can't take Christina away!"

Without thinking of what we were doing, both Dad and I jumped out of the car and raced up to the house.

"You can't come in here," Debby yelled when she spotted us.

"What's going on?" I asked. "Where are you going?"

"Get out of here!" Debby got emotional and kept yelling at me that I didn't have a right to come into the house, that she could do what she wanted and live wherever she wanted to live and that it was none of my business and that she'd call the police if I didn't leave immediately.

Dad was upset and when he tried to get into the house, she yelled at him.

I tried to reason with her, but I think I caught her when she wasn't expecting me. She seemed to react out of guilt because she hadn't told me she was moving. She grew more emotional and I caved in to my own anger, frustration, and fears. Our voices grew louder.

"He's breaking into my house!" she started screaming. "He has no right to be here!"

One of the neighbors called the police.

As soon as the police officer arrived, Debby screamed, "Make him get out of here! He's not supposed to come here!"

I tried to calm her down and I also attemped to explain to the officer that I had just pulled up and discovered she was leaving. "She's taking my daugther, and she didn't tell me!"

It didn't take long to realize that I wasn't getting anywhere. According to the separation papers, I didn't have the right to be at my own house.

"Let's go, Dad," I said sadly. Not waiting for him to answer, I turned and walked to the car.

I was devastated and confused, unable to recollect most of her words. She made it clear she was moving to Aspen, Colorado, and that as soon as the divorce was final she was going to marry Keith Hefner.

And the worst blow—Christina was going with her.

For the next few months, I lived in a fog. Debby, I learned, had confided in most of our friends over the past few months which, of course, I hadn't known, telling them how mean, insensitive, and uncaring I was. I assumed many of them believed her; it didn't matter. I had loved her and lost her. And although I'd be able to visit my daughter, it wouldn't be the same. I had lost Christina too.

After only five years of marriage we went through with the divorce. And almost immediately afterward, Debby married Keith Hefner.

A few people tried to help. Shirley Boone called me and tried to comfort me. She also called Debby shortly before Debby was to marry Keith. I don't know the details of the conversation, but Shirley apparently tried to convince Debby that Debby and I could still work out our differences. Debby made it clear that she had already made her decision, however. Shirley's efforts were futile, but it meant a lot to me to know that someone out there cared enough to try and help.

After the divorce, I faced another hump I had to get over. Many congregations just didn't want a divorced man playing in their churches. Having come from a conservative background, I understood, even though it hurt that they took such a position. I hadn't believed in divorce, had always considered it wrong, and now I was divorced.

The only cure I knew for my pain was to pray a lot and to stay busy. I set up as many concerts as I could for the next few months. I didn't want to think about my life. I wanted to forget the five years of our marriage.

On the road, I never mentioned Debby. If anyone asked about the divorce, I admitted it was true but I didn't talk about it. *I couldn't—it hurt too much.*

I suppose people never suspected that I was in pain. Those who knew about the breakup believed I had everything under control. They didn't have any sense of the tough times I was going through.

Every possible chance, I tried to see Christina. For a while Debby made it difficult for me to see her as often as I would have liked. But I'm sure that came out of her anger toward me—and that didn't last long. After some time passed, Debby became very good about allowing me to see my daughter. She even let me take her on the road or stay with me for short periods.

One day I was relaxing in my hotel after a concert, which is usually a down-time for me anyway. (I throw myself into the program and when I finish, I'm drained.) As I sat in the hotel, I picked up a magazine and thumbed through it but couldn't concentrate on anything I read. I reached for the TV knob and then decided I didn't want to watch anything. "What's wrong with me?" I asked the empty room. "Why can't I get over this divorce?"

Just that quickly, a realization came to me. I thought, *I'm not just hurting over the divorce. This is a multiple hurt.* The Kathryn thing refused to die, and people were still coming around talking about it. A few churches still wouldn't even let me play because of it. Despite my silence, they were still convinced I was out to destroy her reputation.

Then the loss of Debby. I couldn't cut out the love overnight. And coming from my background, loss of family is one of the worst things that can happen.

But the biggest hurt was for Christina. She was only three when Debby and I broke up. Yet we were close, and I loved her very much. My thoughts constantly turned to my daughter, "my little Greek princess." Christina has all the classic Greek features, which makes her look like me. She meant the world to me. From the time she was born I had changed her diapers, rocked her to sleep, and nursed her when she was sick.

I had just finished a concert in Memphis and had been able to have Christina with me.

And as usual, the hardest moment came when I had to take Christina back and say good-bye to her. I hugged her and held her out to friends who were going to take her back to her mother.

"Daddy, Daddy, please, Daddy, I don't want to go, Daddy. I love you, Daddy." With tears in her eyes, my little Christina was wiggling and writhing, doing anything so she wouldn't have to leave me.

Determined not to let her see my own tears flow, I held her again and said softly, "Honey, you have to go. Your mommy is waiting."

It took a long time before she calmed down. Then I walked with her to the car and helped her inside. I nodded for my friends to hurry before Christina started to cry again. They took her to the airport for me because we thought it would be easier if I weren't there.

I stood at the curb and waved, my heart breaking, but I forced myself to keep smiling. I saw her beautiful little face pressed against the window, tears running down her cheeks. Without being aware when they started, I now felt the tears cascading down my own cheeks. The one person I loved most was being pulled away from me. I grieved for her. I grieved for myself.

Chapter 18

THE SINGLE LIFE

"We're not going to let that stop us!" Larry Sparks said, referring to cancellations and rejections because of my divorce. "You have a ministry, a gift. I'll talk to people and I think they'll understand."

"Thanks," I recall saying, wondering if his intervention would do any good. Already depressed over my personal life, I wasn't able to face professional rejection as well.

Larry picked up the phone and started working. He didn't produce results quite as quickly as he had five years earlier, but he did come through. I'm not sure how I would have coped without Larry's help.

In the meantime, I had received an invitation to play for the 1980 summer music conference called the Christian Artists Seminar sponsored by Cam Floria at Estes Park, Colorado. All the big names in Christian music would be around that week from Sandi Patti to Carmany. Besides the seminars, every night they have concerts by various artists and mine was to be one of them.

I still hurt from the loss of Christina, and I didn't want to play at Estes Park. Truthfully, I didn't want to play anywhere. Although I didn't know what I would do, I had considered quitting music altogether. "And the last place in the world I need to be is Estes Park," I told Larry and Cam.

But they persuaded me to go "just for the fellowship."

"OK," I said, "but I'm not sure whether I should play."

Once there, Cam and Larry convinced me to perform. After Cam introduced me, without saying a word I went to the piano. Without backup or other instruments, I began to play "Turn Your Eyes Upon Jesus."

As I played, I sensed that others were feeling my hurt with me, although I hadn't talked about it. As my fingers moved over the keys, I prayed, *You know, God, I'm not good with words and I can't tell these people how bad I'm hurting. Help me say it through my music. Use this medium to communicate my pain and to give them healing for their own pain.*

I can only say that in my playing, in my self-offering, God started the healing process in my own heart. As I stared at the keyboard, my fingers were pouring out all my pain and handing it to God as an offering.

Naturally, I had no idea what God was doing to the audience, and I'm not sure it made much difference to me at that moment. I was throwing myself on God's mercy in the way I communicate best—through this special gift God has given to me.

A man from Washington, D.C., named Harry Causey sat near the front with his wife. Harry had never heard of me before and when I walked up to the stage, his first impression of me was negative—I was wearing a blue tuxedo. That was enough for Harry to know that he already didn't like me, and he knew he wasn't going to enjoy the performance. All kinds of things went through his mind . . . *he's a Liberace flash; he's a phony; he's just trying to look fancy.*

When I started to play, something startling took place inside of Harry. As I poured out my heart to God through my fingers, a change took place in Harry.

"I went in there not liking you and wasn't going to like you," he later told me. "Then as you played, God took over and broke my spirit. I felt all the hurt and the pain in my own life. I no longer saw you as some flashy character up there, but I understood that you are a man who knows sadness and hurt." We connected.

Since then, Harry Causey's telling of that incident has made him one of my most faithful PR people. Harry did understand. And his understanding helped to make the experience worthwhile.

Through the years, my desire has been for my music to speak to others as it did that night to Harry. When I play concerts I talk to people on a one-to-one basis as much as I can. But what's in my heart comes out in my piano playing. I pray that the listeners will feel my message and sense my concern and caring.

This music is not just for Christians but for all people. Occasionally, I get more non-Christians at my concerts than church people because they like the music, especially the classical pieces and those like "Chariots of Fire." I like to think that they sense my warmth and care.

During my concerts I also take the opportunity to tell them about my relationship to Jesus Christ. God called me and I value my ministry. It's a different ministry, and no one else does it quite this way, but it's the only way I know to do it.

For years I wanted to give a piano away—perhaps because when we were poor, I got started on a piano a Greek friend gave my mother. My idea for a white grand piano giveaway first came when I played in Pianorama, a concert to encourage young pianists. The concert premiered on "PTL." I started with five pianos and then moved up to seven, all Baldwin grand pianos. We placed six black pianos in a kind of semicircle around my white piano. Three men and three women played the black pianos, while I played the white piano in the center. We had a musical treat.

That's when Baldwin began to build white pianos for me. And they have been kind to me ever since. Wherever I play, they place one of their pianos at the auditorium for my use. They view it as advertisement for both the Baldwin pianos and the Baldwin artist.

In the early 1980s Baldwin bought my idea for the white grand piano giveaway. "White not only looks good," I joked, "but it looks like a Christian piano." The idea to use white may have come to me as a reminder of Kathryn, because she often wore white. But the most obvious reason was that white stood out on stage.

Everybody could enter this annual contest by sending in his or her name and address. Local Baldwin dealers advertised it as the Great White Piano Giveaway. On a television show, I picked a name at random from a barrel. This has become a highlight of my tour every year.

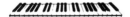

My life was moving along. I saw Christina whenever I could and I increased the number of concerts. By 1984 I was doing about two hundred a year. I was still lonely but keeping busy helped.

Being single seemed to make me the target for all kinds of stories. Some whispered I was a homosexual. My guess is that because of my "dash of flash," they sometimes compared me to Liberace. He was a known homosexual so people must have figured I was too. Or sometimes the stories circulated that I was having an affair with some woman.

In 1981 I played a concert in Springfield, Illinois, and stayed in a hotel. When I checked out the next day, the clerk charged me for two people staying in the room.

"This amount isn't correct," I said, and asked the desk clerk to make the change.

The desk clerk had just assumed that I had a woman in my room and charged me accordingly. He didn't ask; he didn't verify.

I had slept in the room alone.

Because of his assumption and somebody talking without knowing facts, a rumor circulated around the church where I had played the night before that a woman had spent the night in my room. When I heard about it, I told Paul, who had started to work for me, "Please call that hotel and clarify that situation."

The hotel manager apologized, but I insisted he had to do more. "Insist that he phone the local pastor and tell him the truth."

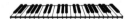

People with serious psychological problems sometimes attend my concerts. One day I received a subpoena to go to court in Wisconsin. The woman plaintiff claimed that I came to her town every two weeks and conducted an ongoing affair with her.

She also claimed that I held a gun to her head and raped her—a really unbelievable thing. Paul had to hire an attorney for me. The attorney proved beyond question that on the alleged dates, I was playing concerts in other parts of the country and could not possibly have been there.

After a brief investigation, they learned that the woman was under psychiatric care. The court system had never checked on any of the facts when she filed the suit.

Strange. Weird. And it takes so much energy as well as time and expense to cope with these things.

Occasionally I get mail from women with unusual romantic notions, and sometimes they sound dangerous. One woman wrote that she and I were having an affair "in our spirits." She had frequently attended my concerts and hinted that she'd like to move from the spiritual realm into the region of the flesh!

With things like this happening, it's easy to understand why many entertainers have bodyguards. As we've learned in recent years, a strange person could come along with a gun and do something harmful. I don't worry about those things, though I try not to do anything foolish.

Another reality of being a concert artist is the encounters I have with mothers (or more rarely, fathers or other family members) who drag their children to my dressing room.

"I'm sorry to bother you, Dino," she'll invariably say, "but tell him—tell him how long he should practice."

What do I say? I stare at the child, usually a kid who probably hates the piano to start with. So I joke a little and say, "Oh, about ten minutes." Then before Mama goes into hysterics, I say, "Listen, at least a half hour of concentrated practice ought to be plenty."

"Dino, how long do you practice? Tell him that!" And Mama smiles triumphantly, assured I'm going to say ten hours.

"That varies," I say, trying to avoid giving a figure. "When I'm on the road, I don't practice much . . ."

"But when you're home? How long then?"

Trapped, I respond, "Remember, I'm a professional. This is my calling, and this is how I earn my living. When I'm working on a new album, I'll put in ten to fifteen hours of practice a day. From morning till night when I'm learning new music and new material, but . . ."

It doesn't matter what I say after that to try to explain. Ambitious Mama has her answer.

"See!" she'll squeal with the glow of victory and haul the poor kid back down the hallway.

On the other hand, when I spot an alert child during one of my concerts and ask, "Do you play the piano?" and get an affirmative answer, I then say, "Come on up here and play the piano."

The kid will sit down at a white Baldwin grand piano and play. And the audience has never let me down when the child finishes. The applause is wonderful. Each time I think, *This may be launching the career of a talented pianist.*

I want to encourage young people to develop the ability God has given them, whether it's piano playing, singing, dancing, or playing a sport. One reason I made it professionally is because of the people who believed in me and encouraged me.

Then another tragedy struck. Dad died February 4, 1985. He'd had heart trouble for years, but I suppose I never thought much about losing him. Then he was gone.

I didn't realize how much I loved my dad till I saw him lying in the casket. He had turned out to be a strong Christian in the last years of his life, and we had grown close.

I stared at his lifeless form in the casket and thought of so many things. In particular, I remembered that whenever

I was exhausted from being on the road alone, caught up in one of the hardships, I frequently called him. "I'm fine, Dad, but I'm tired, just worn out and not sure I can make it."

He'd listen to all my troubles and then he'd say to me in Greek, "Dino, just keep serving Jesus. Don't give up. Just keep serving Jesus."

But it's different now, I thought, as my eyes moistened. *He's gone. I'll never hear his encouraging words again.* Then, from somewhere deep inside me, I plainly heard Dad's voice say, "Keep serving Jesus. Don't give up."

Tears flooded me and right then, beside Dad's casket, I recommitted my life to Jesus Christ. "Dear Lord," I said, "I rededicate my life and talent to serve You until I see You in person."

That experience put me on another level in my ministry. Even today, when I find myself going down, I can pause and listen. Faintly, very faintly, I hear those words again, "Keep serving Jesus."

I always answer, "I will, Dad. I won't give up."

Chapter 19

THE RIGHT WOMAN

"Who is *she*?" I asked, trying to sound casual.

I had come to premiere my new album, *Regal Reign,* at the official opening of the Dinner Theater of the Grand Hotel connected with Jim Bakker's PTL television station. They had organized the opening with all the glitter of a major Hollywood film premier.

"Who?" Maude Aimee Humbard answered.

"The one with the dark hair. Who is she?"

Maude Aimee is a sharp lady and she picked up on more than my question. "Her name is Cheryl. She's Gary McSpadden's sister." Almost everyone connected with the gospel music field knew the McSpadden family. Cheryl's brother Gary had sung with the Bill Gaither Trio. Her father, Boyd McSpadden, has the reputation of being an excellent preacher and is highly respected.

"She's beautiful!"

"You leave her alone," Maude Aimee whispered. "Get your eyes back inside your head and behave. She's going with a nice fellow. So she's off limits."

"I can at least appreciate beauty, can't I?"

"I know you Greeks!" she said with a smile. "She *is* pretty, isn't she?"

"Breathtaking." I continued to stare.

My inner healing had begun five years earlier at the music conference in Estes Park. By 1985, I had gone through all the stages of grief and pain. My career was progressing. But one void remained. Deep inside, I knew I wasn't the kind of person who could live the single life indefinitely. I needed a wife; I needed companionship.

Yet God's will in my life came first. If I married again, she would be God's choice for me. And she would be the right kind of woman—one who would be my companion and not a person compelled to compete or who attempted to dominate.

I didn't go out looking for a wife. If God wanted me to have a wife, I believed he would bring us together.

Then, on January 1, 1985, I saw a beautiful woman. She was so breathtakingly attractive, I found myself staring at her black hair and vibrant hazel eyes. She wore a hot-pink silk dress, and I thought, *This woman could be a top model.* She had that fine bone structure possessed by women who are naturally beautiful.

Mike, the man she was with, brought her to our table and introduced her to me, the Humbards, Tammy Bakker, and the others. Then they moved on and sat at a table near us. Other than being introduced, I had no chance to talk to her. Even worse, I didn't see her the rest of the time I was there.

Half a year later, I saw Cheryl for the second time. On July 4, 1985, again at the PTL, I saw Cheryl sitting with a group of people I knew. After going over to their table and chatting a few minutes, I said to them all, while I was looking directly at Cheryl, "I'm playing at the Dinner Theater tomorrow night. Would everybody here be guests at my table? I'd like to have the whole group."

"We'd like that," someone said and another voiced his pleasure at being invited. At that moment I wanted to say something to the beautiful woman named Cheryl, but just

then Tammy Bakker asked me a question, and I became
involved in conversation with her. Before I had a chance to
break away, Cheryl was gone.

As I would learn later, Cheryl had been going through a
difficult period in her life. After nineteen years of marriage,
she had gone through a divorce and was still learning to
readjust.

The next evening, just before I started to play, my eyes
swept across the audience and I smiled. Cheryl sat next to
JoAnn Pflug, the actress who had starred in the movie version of M*A*S*H and in a variety of television films. To her
left was Judah Ranier of the famous car-racing family. But it
was Cheryl, of course, who grabbed my attention.

The concert went smoothly; I sensed that I had played
extraordinarily well. Just as I finished my encore, I leaned
toward the vase of long-stemmed roses on the corner of
the piano, pulled out a single rose, and tossed it to Cheryl.
Unfortunately, my aim wasn't perfect and Judah Ranier,
who is a wildly funny woman, grabbed the rose and
squealed in delight.

A few minutes later I came to the table and Judah made a
joke about my throwing the rose at her. "And me a married
woman!" She laughed, obviously having fun teasing me.

"I meant the rose for Cheryl," I said.

"Oh, and I thought you were flirting with me!" Judah
laughed loudly.

Cheryl didn't say anything; she just gave me a smile.

The Bakkers had arranged a reception in the restaurant.
Because the atmosphere was fairly casual and comfortable,
I did some moving around. I was delighted that Cheryl was
present for the reception, and twice I tried to get close
enough to talk to her. Since the Bakkers had given the reception in my honor, they, as good hosts, focused the attention on me for the evening.

I sat next to Tammy Bakker, who is an impressive con-
versationalist. She told us one funny story after another. We

all laughed and I barely listened as Tammy started telling us another incident. From the corner of my eye, I watched Cheryl get up from her table and walk in our direction. When she reached our table, I beamed as I stood.

"Excuse me," Cheryl said, "but I did want to tell you, Dino, how much I enjoyed your music and how I appreciated your invitation this evening."

I acknowledged her thanks and said, "Sit down and talk with us a few minutes."

She sat down and while I was trying to think of what to say next, Tammy launched into a hilarious story about a mixed-up phone call at PTL. Occasionally Cheryl or I said something, but Tammy, having a grand time, kept us laughing.

After a few minutes, Cheryl got up, told me again how much my music had touched her, and started to leave the room.

I couldn't think of what to say to keep her from leaving, and I panicked. "Uh, before you go," I blurted out, "where do you live?"

"Nashville."

"Really?" By now Nashville was *the* place for gospel recording. "I'm in Nashville a lot. Maybe we could get together. Uh, maybe sometime we can have lunch together." I surprised myself in being so forward because I'd been out of the dating game a long time.

"That would be nice," she said. I liked the softness of her voice. I decided she was even prettier than I had thought when I first saw her six months earlier.

My own words sounded hollow, and I could just imagine her thinking sarcastically, *Oh, sure, Dino.* What I said sounded like the typical line people in the music business use. "Let's keep in touch" or "Let's do lunch," but the words usually mean nothing. As she left, I thought, *She probably assumes I say that to everybody.*

After she was gone, the obvious struck me: *Dino, you didn't ask for her telephone number.* I slapped my forehead in disgust. I wanted to talk to her to find out how involved she was with the other man. She wasn't wearing an engagement ring, which gave me the impression that it wasn't that serious. But if she were committed to him, I wouldn't try to interfere.

Unknown to me, after returning to Nashville, Cheryl decided she wanted to prepare herself to be of greater service to Jesus Christ. Entering a Bible college seemed the right thing so she planned to move to Dallas and attend Christ for the Nations International Bible College (CFNI) established by the late Gordon Lindsay and his wife, Freda. A natural choice, as she had known the Lindsay family all her life. As children, Cheryl and their youngest son, Dennis, who is now the president of the college, played together. Cheryl had a daughter named Cheri, who was seventeen, and she would be enrolling in Trinity Christian Academy in Dallas.

I tried to find Cheryl's telephone number in Nashville but had no luck until my friend, Linda Hilliard, said she knew Cheryl. "We used to go to the same church, and I think she moved to Texas," she said. "We didn't know each other very well though."

"Any chance you could find out where she is now?"

"Probably," Linda said. She knew Mike, the man Cheryl had been dating the first time I saw her. "Seems to me they broke up," she said, "but I'll call him. He ought to know where she's living."

Mike's secretary gave Linda the number, and I asked Linda to call Cheryl for me.

"I'm working for Dino Kartsonakis," she told Cheryl. "That's why I'm phoning you. Dino asked me to call you to ask you if it was all right if he called you."

"Linda, are you serious?" Cheryl asked. "You called to find out if it was OK for him to call?"

Linda laughed. "That's right."

"My goodness, he must be a true gentleman."

"He is." Linda then explained that I didn't want to call if she was involved with anyone.

"That sounds like a lovely, wonderful, genteel thing to do," Cheryl said. "Yes, I'd be delighted for him to call."

Within thirty minutes, I phoned Cheryl and we chatted easily enough. Cheryl told me about her move to Dallas and her desire to serve God. Before hanging up, I said, "I'm going to be in Dallas next week. How about dinner?"

"I'd like to get it straight, right up front," she said. "I want you to know I'm not interested in a relationship. I don't want a relationship with anybody. I'm in school and planning to go into some form of ministry. I'm going to sing and do the things my heart has desired all these years. Now if you just want to go out to dinner and have a nice conversation, I'd like that. Frankly, I could sure stand some adult conversation."

"That's all I want too," I said. As much as I wanted to find a woman I could love, I was still a little scared. "Right now I'm not quite ready for a new relationship either."

The following week I flew into Dallas. Cheri was home so I met her before we left. Cheryl and I had dinner at a lovely restaurant. Unfortuantely, Cheryl had a terrible cold and was obviously suffering. She didn't want to cough or blow her nose at the table, so she excused herself and went to the ladies' room. However, the ladies' room was a long way from the table and each time she left, it took five minutes before she returned. This happened three times.

When she came back the third time, I said, "Now level with me. You don't have a cold. You have a real kidney problem."

She burst into laughter.

That little joke broke down the reserve between us. From then on, we enjoyed a pleasant evening together.

And I also knew I liked her better than anyone I had met in a long time.

I took her home after dinner. Not sure if I should kiss her or shake her hand, in my nervousness, I simply said, "I'll call you." As I drove off, I said to myself, "Dino, that sounded like the all-time dumb statement of your life."

But I did mean it. I intended to call her again. Often.

A few days later, I called her. "I'll be in Dallas Thursday. Let's do lunch."

"Yes," she said, "I'd like that."

We went to lunch. Then we went to dinner again. Every time I saw Cheryl I liked her more. From then on, I kept finding excuses to fly into Dallas. Occasionally, Cheryl skipped a class or two so we could have lunch. The more I saw her, the more I wanted to be with her.

Then I realized something else—I had fallen in love with Cheryl. The more I prayed about the two of us, the more at peace I felt. "God, I believe You sent Cheryl into my life. If that's right, help me be sure and help her too."

By then I was flying in and out of Dallas twice a week, occasionally squeezing in a third trip.

After a few more weeks of this commuting, one evening when we went out, I said, "I love you."

"Oh, Dino, don't," she answered. "I'm scared. I don't want to hear anything more . . ."

"I love you, Cheryl."

"Please don't say that. You're the most wonderful person I've ever met, and I thoroughly enjoy being with you, but . . ."

"But what?"

"I'm still frightened of a new relationship. I had one difficult marriage, and I'm not about to jump into a second one."

"That makes sense and I certainly understand," I said. "I'll wait."

During the next few weeks, I knew it was going to be all right. We both prayed about our relationship. Another neat feature about going out with Cheryl—we prayed together at the end of every date. Although I had dated Christian girls, I had never felt comfortable enough to pray with them.

One night after we had been out to dinner, we parked outside her apartment. We talked quite a long time, and then we started to pray. Right in the middle of our praying, the campus security guard came around, saw us parked, and walked over. He flashed his light into our eyes. I felt embarrassed as I thought about our being two mature people, sitting in a car parked on a college campus late at night. From a distance, we must have looked like two young kids.

"Let me see some ID," he said matter-of-factly.

I started laughing, and Cheryl handed him her student ID card.

He read the information, stared at her and shook his head slowly. Finally he said, "What are you doing here?"

"Studying," Cheryl answered.

"Oh." The guard moved on.

"Cheryl, what are you really doing in school?" I asked her.

"Like I told the security guard, studying . . ."

"You're a preacher's daughter, you've been in church all your life, you've been involved in some form of ministry all your life. You really know the Bible," I said. "No, Cheryl, I think you're here to escape from life."

"I'm here to learn!" she protested.

"Cheryl, you're hiding here." I hadn't thought about that before, but the words popped out. As I said them, I knew they were true.

"I want to study the Bible. I want to . . ." she stopped, thinking about what I had said. "You know, Dino, maybe you're right."

"I know I am."

Cheryl hadn't been intentionally hiding or running away but as soon as I pointed this out to her, she realized I was right. "I guess I am hiding. When I came here, I desperately wanted security, something safe to hold on to. During those years of marriage, I lost my sense of security and self-assurance. I've found it again by being here."

"Then isn't it time to move on?"

"Oh, Dino, I don't know . . ."

"Yes, you do," I told her softly.

As we continued to talk, Cheryl admitted that she had found what she had been seeking. At school, in prayer meetings, in being with other believers, in simply being around people who accepted her and who also wanted to serve God, she had found herself and gained a new sense of confidence. Thoughts raced through her head, giving her new insights.

"You know, Dino," she said. "At last I've become an individual, my own person. Like other women I know, I had gone from my parents' house to my husband's. He was my husband, but in some ways it was like another daddy because I married so young. Now that's changed. I'm on my own and responsible for myself and for my daughter."

"Then why don't you quit hiding?" I asked again. "I love you." I could feel knots in my stomach, but I finished what I wanted to say. "You don't want to admit it, but I know you love me too."

"Oh, Dino . . ."

"You do love me, Cheryl. Let's get married."

"Get married?"

"Yeah. You know . . . men and women do this all the time."

"I can't get married," she said, and I could tell the words had shocked her because I was pushing things fast. "I've got school to finish. I've got Cheri to think about, and I can't just up and get married like a teenager."

"No, you can't," I said, "but we can work it out. If you want to." I paused and stared at her in the semidarkness.

"I do love you," Cheryl admitted for the first time. "I know that much."

"OK, tell you what," I said. "Let's talk to everybody involved in your decision. Let's start here at the Bible College with Mrs. Lindsay and find out if our getting married is OK with her. If she gives us her blessing, then we'll talk to your parents. And to Cheri, of course. If all of them give their blessing, then let's get married."

"All right," she agreed.

From that moment, neither of us had doubts about loving each other and wanting to spend the rest of our lives together. As we had agreed, we went to Cheri to ask her blessing. When we told her, she rather calmly said, "Well, it's about time, isn't it?"

Cheri and I had established a rapport with one another when we first met, and we had become good friends through my time of dating Cheryl. I had believed she would be excited about our marriage plans, but I was aware of the potential difficulties and adjustments that lay ahead of her. Cheri seemed free to release her mother to a new marriage, however, though it would mean Cheryl's leaving to travel with me while Cheri lived with a family in Dallas in order to complete her high school education.

Despite the pain Cheri experienced as a young person, she has displayed a strength and maturity which I've admired since I've known her. We have, through the years, continued to grow closer. Cheri calls me Dad and relates to me as if I were her natural father, and she has become like a blood sister to Christina. Cheryl and I are thankful for both of our girls; and we couldn't have asked for an easier, more natural transition into a second marriage, a new family.

Next we went to Mrs. Lindsay's office. She questioned us first. "Tell me about your marriage and divorce, Dino," she said. As I talked, she interrupted occasionally to clarify something I had said. Then she had a number of questions of her own, mainly about my commitment to Jesus Christ.

Then, for nearly an hour, she counseled us about marriage. Finally she said, "I think I know about both of your lives and your pasts. Yes, I think God is putting you two together."

I flew Cheryl's parents, Boyd and Helen McSpadden, into Dallas so I could meet them and ask for their blessing. They met me at Cheryl's apartment. They wanted to know about me, and we talked for a long time.

"You're sure about this?" Boyd McSpadden turned to Cheryl. "You're really sure this is the man for you?"

"I've never been so sure of anything before," she said.

"And, Dino, you're just as sure this is God's will?" Helen McSpadden asked.

"I've known almost from the time we starting dating," I answered truthfully. "I love her."

"Then we give you both our blessings," Cheryl's father said.

Cheryl had already met my little Christina at PTL, but she didn't really know her. As the two of them got better acquainted, they really took to each other.

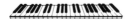

Before Cheryl and I met, I had bought a condo in Dallas as an investment. After we had started to talk marriage I said, "Why don't we make this our dream place?" The condo was close to Cheri's school, and Cheryl arranged for Cheri to finish her last year in high school by boarding with her close friend, Charlotte, and her family near the school. This arrangement gave Cheryl the freedom to travel with me, something we both wanted.

Cheryl liked the idea. I have a good friend who is a talented decorator. He and his wife decorated the place exactly to Cheryl's taste with beautiful Grecian columns and chandeliers, antique furniture, and everything done in grays and mauves.

We married December 26, 1985, in the condo with family and a few select friends present. Our daughters were Cheryl's attendants and two of my nephews stood with me. We had a ministerial staff of four: Cheryl's brother, Gary McSpadden; her father; Paul Bartholomew; and Don George, the pastor of Calvary Temple in Dallas.

At last, I had finally found her—my wife. I've been through a lot of ups and downs, but I've now received a special blessing—Cheryl. Together we're serving the Lord. She supports my ministry of communicating God's love and peace through music.

Of all the miracles God has performed in my life, Cheryl is the best.